Mick Allan

CYCLORAMA   1 »

Jim McGurn and Mick Allan

» **We hope you'll enjoy Cyclorama.** There was only so much we could squeeze into a book of this size, so we have also created an international online resource on cycling. We have been building this up over several years, and it has a hundred times the content of this book. It also gives lots more information on the cycles and cycle-makers which are 'case-studied' in this book (and we list their own websites on page 158). Please visit **www.cyclorama.net** It gives you more than any printed book can offer!

Bicycle parked outside a coffee
shop downtown, Portland
Image: Ryan Heyne

Contents »

The answers come with pedals on »

It's not long since we first learned to balance on an arrangement of metal tubes and a pair of skinny wheels. We made ourselves the motor, an amazing bio-engine which improves its own strength and efficiency – and even its working life – the more it's used. We suddenly became the most beautiful movers in the known universe.

If bikes are so good, why are they not everywhere? Perhaps they're too cheap, too simple, too universal, too harmless for their own good. Perhaps they're becoming too free of status markers for those who find these things important. Bikes are a form of independent and virtually uncontrollable private transport which are very often at odds with every other road transport system, including buses. Perhaps the problem is that bikes require us to make our bodies do something useful. We've spent a

century scrapping manual jobs, and turning professional sport into a spectator activity. Personal fitness is still a major aspiration, but is now packaged as a consumer item, to be enjoyed in private gyms and expensive leisure centres. To keep fit while you have fun just transporting yourself around is so sensible it verges, in some societies, on the subversive.

The bicycle is perfect at converting our metabolic energy into kinetic energy. On a bicycle we can go three or four times faster than on foot, but use five times less energy in the process. Equipped with this tool we outstrip the efficiency of not only all machines, but all other animals as well.

The bicycle testifies to the importance and beauty of the human body, that incredibly efficient constant-temperature fuel cell. It takes us where we want to go fast, and makes streets great places to be, rather than to travel through. The cry goes up to get teenagers off the street. But that's exactly where they should be.

It's where we all should be. Enjoying our streets and communities. Instead we've opted for private, internalised pleasures. Beautiful rooms, in our hide-away houses. The cabin-calm of the luxury motor car, hermetically sealed off from the world outside, with all its threatening confusion, weirdness and identity challenges – a environment in which cyclists can find happiness and community.

The arguments for cycling have long since been won, but many of us are in a hole, having to live within 'communities' with facilities spaced out at car-driving distances. There is no paradise round the corner. Road cycling is a no-go area for many who are anxious or inexperienced. Many cycle paths are for leisure use, and do little for commuters. Many governments are still failing to take cycling seriously, denying a basic freedom to millions.

Twin-track policies will not go far. Promoting cycling comes to natural limits if nothing is done about motor traffic. There seems to be a sentiment abroad that all will be well once the boffins come up with cleaner fuel. This is the stuff of fantasy. Even the cleanest 'eco-cars', if they ever come about, will still kill and maim, demanding roads which distort and destroy communities.

The bicycle comes in many forms, because our needs are complex. There are now astonishing lightweight city bikes, ingenious folding bikes for mixed-mode travel, load-carrying cycles for bringing home the shopping, robust tandems for fetching your visitors from the station, multi-seaters for riding *en famille*, electric-assist bikes for that extra energy, and sleek recumbents for going faster in more comfort. Alongside all of this the new generations of performance road bikes and MTBs take technology to new heights. The pedal-powered solutions are out there now, ready to make a difference to many different parts of our lives. **Jim McGurn**

 There is no other invention than the bicycle which so intimately combines the useful with the enjoyable "

Adam Opel (1837-95) Industrialist

Vintage and Retro »

Brand new bicycles from the good old days

» RetroVelo Paul, Germany

The bicycle industry is obsessed with new technology. And it always has been. Advances in materials technology, manufacturing processes, ergonomics and function are what drive the wheels of the bicycle world around. It is the never ending quest for performance advantage which has delivered us the amazing range of light, reliable and easy to use bikes we all ride today. With very few exceptions, the history of the bicycle is not one of great big innovations and giant steps. It's a long story, a slow whittling away of superfluous weight, a tweak here, a fine tune there. Evolution rather than revolution.

The bicycle departments of the world's transport museums record the slow development of our favourite mode, the design cul-de-sacs, the failed innovations. The bad ideas. There have been some very bad ideas. We modern cyclists stand at our particular point in the history of the bicycle looking to the future, awaiting the latest developments with bated breath. But modern, top of the range bikes with their electronic shifting, carbon nano-tube frames and hollow chainrings disguise a fundamental truth – there's not much new under the sun. Some of the things we think of as modern inventions are no such thing.

Aluminum frames? 1890s. Butted frame tubing? 1897. Dual suspension? 1915. And as for disc wheels – the pinnacle of high-tech aerodynamic speed weaponry – they've been around since the 1880s. Invented to keep ladies' skirts out of their spokes!

Bicycle designs and fashions come and go, but a very few machines have remained in production in spite of the passage of time. By virtue of their classic status or the sheer brilliance of their conception a tiny handful of designs have survived and can be purchased today. Replica high wheeled 'penny farthings' are still being produced by a few dedicated craftsmen dotted around the globe. Pedersen's astonishingly beautiful hammock-saddled design remains in production – fundamentally unchanged - over a century after its conception. These rare, unusual, outstanding designs have inspired a tiny handful of artisans to keep them alive, but the phenomenon tells us little about the mainstream. What of ordinary bikes for ordinary people?

Bicycle magazines are full of the latest gizmos, latest trends and next year's models, when – let's be honest – there was nothing wrong with the bikes which were in the shops last year. The market being what it is, each manufacturer has to be seen to be on the leading edge lest they give the fickle consumer the impression that they are being left behind.

Some manufacturers, however, play a different game. But they're not being left behind, simply playing by their own rules.

The enormous resurgence of cycling in our major cities is a result of new people adopting cycling. But what the industry categorises as new cyclists are almost never completely new. Many will be returning to the fold after years on other modes of travel. When these folks step out of their trains and cars and approach cycling afresh they have no knowledge of the latest technology. The last time they rode a bike was ten, twenty, thirty years ago. They have no desire to understand the difference between 6061-T6 and 7005 series aluminium. They don't want team replica paint schemes or zillion-speed gizmotronic

» Dawes Cambridge

transmissions. They want simplicity, they want ease of use and they want comfort. They want a bicycle which puts them in mind – not of hi-viz jackets and rush hour traffic or Hat-on-Back-to-Front Mountain Mayhem Tattooed Extreme Team – but of English summer meadows, bunting, afternoon tea and lemon cake. They want a bike like the one Mamma used to ride. They want a bike which speaks to their soul.

And they want a wicker basket. If that's not too much to ask.

Large parts of the mainstream cycling industry are inward looking and insular. Populated by bike geeks and in thrall to the march of technology they neglected the people who wanted to buy ordinary utility bikes for a generation. They churned out bikes which simply weren't attractive to many new cyclists who wanted style combined with practicality. Though, credit where it's due, the Germans, Dutch and Danes kept the flame alive, making simple but classy bikes for ordinary people and their everyday journeys.

Today, in some parts of the world, 'Retro' bikes are the fastest growing sector of the market. But they're not exactly like the bikes of old. Thank goodness. In the 'good old days', before aluminium rims and lightweight tubing, most bikes weighed as much as a garden shed and had the stopping distance of an oil tanker in the wet. It wasn't enough to simply re-manufacture those old models. Forward-looking manufacturers have looked backward for inspiration, taken classic designs and retro styling, and combined them with modern materials and technology like sealed bearings and aluminium components. Creating attractive bikes which are also good to ride – the best of both worlds. You can have your cake – and eat it too.

» Bella by Beg, England

» Corinto by Taurus Biciclette, Italy

T-Model Pedersen Manufaktur »

Pedersen Manufaktur are devoted specialists. They've been in the business of selling Pedersen bikes and accessories since 1991 and strive to keep their machines in touch with the latest technological developments within the cycle industry, without losing sight of Mikael Pedersen's original vision. Originally produced in Denmark, in 2002 they moved production of their frames to the Czech Republic. The bikes are assembled by Roland Werk in Germany and range from fully equipped, ready-for-the-road machines based around stock frame sizes to individual custom builds. So confident are they of the superiority of Pedersen's iconic bicycle that they offer free week-long test rides. Customers within Germany pay only shipping, a token fee which is returned if the customer later buys a bike. Most do.

One of the world's few departures from mainstream cycle design was the brainchild of Mikael Pedersen. In an age of febrile innovation this prolific and inventive Dane produced, among other things, a corn thresher, a gearing system for horse-driven mills, one of the earliest geared bicycle hubs and a braking system for wagons. Pedersen was also involved in the development of a continuous centrifuge for the churning and separation of cream and butter from milk. When R A Lister and Co of Dursley, Gloucestershire, wanted to set up a local assembly operation with parts shipped from Denmark, Pedersen moved to England. The separator was enormously successful in his adopted country, and he became very wealthy. He rented the largest house in Dursley and became a prominent local dignitary. He formed a choir, took part in concerts, and established a number of social and sporting groups. Pedersen, loved cycling, but was unhappy with the comfort of the bicycle saddles of the day, so he famously invented the hammock saddle and designed the frame around it. He obtained a patent for his unique cantilever frame

» Mikael and Dagmar Pedersen

bicycle in 1893 and persuaded the Lister Company to establish a production line to manufacture it. Following some spectacular sporting successes — including the Bristol to London record — the Pedersen earned a devoted following, but overall fewer than 8,000 bikes were produced. Versions included ladies' models, track racers and tandems.

Pedersen was a spend-thrift who lacked business sense and was prone to being cheated. In his sixties he secretly slipped away from Dursley, leaving his family behind. A friend spotted him selling matches on a London street, and kindly arranged to pay his ticket back to Denmark, in 1920. Pedersen died there nine years later, penniless and unknown, and was buried in a pauper's grave in Copenhagen.

The Pedersen bicycle's inherent advantages have caused it to remain in commercial production, supported by a client base of enthusiasts. It is also bought by complete strangers to the concept, who simply fall in love with the striking design and the comfort of the ride.

In 1995 a collection was started by a group of Pedersen bicycle enthusiasts to raise funds in order to bring Mikael Pedersen's remains back to Dursley and re-bury them there. The service was led by the Bishop of Gloucester and attended by over 300 people including representatives from the Danish Embassy and Pedersen's grandchildren. Refined versions of his milk separating centrifuge are in use to this day. As are his bicycles.

« Pedersen
Kemper Fahrradtechnik

Michael Kemper has been making Pedersen frames for 25 years. He makes them to order, so they fit the customer exactly, with all components and accessories as the client requires. Orders come from around the world and no two are the same.

Alongside these bespoke cycles Michael offers 'customised' Pedersens based on the classic design and adjustable for anyone with an inside leg of 80 cm to 90 cm. Particularly important with Pedersens is the angle of the saddle, which is variable and can be exactly adjusted.

Customers who do not need a bespoke Pedersen can, in this way, still have a Pedersen bicycle which is exactly right for them. They have a choice of Shimano Alfine 8-speed, Alfine 11 and Rohloff. This clever way of meeting all needs means that almost all customers can have their perfect machine: for any kind of riding: from afternoon joyride to serious touring.

Taurus ▌▌█
Contropedale »

The Contropedale is a classic design of the utmost simplicity. Aluminum components make it less attractive to the forces of gravity than the vintage machinery it so closely resembles. With a single speed coaster brake there are no cables to clutter the lines and the two obvious concessions to practicality only enhance the bike's good looks. Pinstriped mudguards and an old fashioned chaincase keep the spray off the rider's back and the oil on the chain where it belongs.

Mesicek ◣
High Bicycle »

When Josef Mesicek first discovered a battered but original high bicycle he took it apart and rebuilt it for youngsters in his local cycling club. But one bike did not go very far among 64 members, so Josef decided to produce another. And another...
Making high bicycles quickly became a hobby, then a passion, and before long a business. Josef and his son Zdenek construct their own high-wheelers by combining various design elements of the original high bicycle. A team of four work in their workshop, hand-fashioning every component to their very exacting standards. Nothing is rushed.

« Retrovelo ▬
Paula

Retrovelo see themselves as inheritors of a local tradition of craftsmanship and design. They are inspired by styles of bike which were common in their region — not so much for reasons of retro fashion, but because they see these classic cycles as a part of who they are and want to be. They seek cultural continuity and authenticity and can trace unbroken family histories of bicycles, even across continents, such as the influence of German designers in the early US Schwinns, carried there by immigrants.

For them, 'retro' means a return to values of genuine quality and purity of design. The Paula, like all of their bikes, is the product of these values: comfortable, stylish and built to last a lifetime.

Good old-fashioned utility bikes are finding new popularity in many countries. As a result an awareness of the practical benefits of bicycle baskets is on the way back up. An essential accessory on our grandmothers' bicycles, the humble bicycle basket is also perfect for the modern urbane cyclist. Made right, baskets are lightweight and extremely durable. As if that's not enough, they are also easily recyclable, made from sustainable materials and support craftspeople and their communities. The people at the Nantucket Bike Basket Co. source their handsome baskets from all over the world, making them in traditional materials — rattan and willow — and in many different styles. Some are inspired by fishermen's baskets of the 1800s: surely making them one of the few ancient things which still have a place in the modern world.

Nantucket Bike Basket Co. »

How the bicycle pedalled to perfection

Long journeys of the mind took us from rolling boulders and tree trunks to gliding about, feet off the ground, on a couple of wheels held together by a neat little collection of sticks formed into triangles.

For thousands of years we transported ourselves and our few tools using the most efficient and adaptive machine of all: our bodies, and a pair of shoes is still a pretty clever thing to have. But our forefathers must have looked at the dynamics of other objects in daily life, and seen how a child's play hoop stays upright, how skaters balance in-line on sharpened deer antlers. The idea of balance on two wheels probably came from many sources, and who knows how many times in history a two-wheeler was invented for a bit of fun, then lost from human memory.

Strands of human-powered technology were later to intertwine. The concept of balls in bearings, so cleverly set out by daVinci, was to be perfected centuries later in the development of the bicycle, and applied to the wheels of roller skates. Developments never cease: in-line skating on modern urban surfaces comes close to matching the efficiency of the bicycle, and is sometimes more convenient.

1 » From servant-power to serious play

We harnessed other animals, as external power sources for our land transport. Very early attempts to replace horse-power with human-power resulted in heavy four-wheeled carriages powered by servants pressing on treadles or cranked axles, while their lord and master sat up front steering the monster around his country estate. Who knows, it may have been a great amusement for all concerned, as well as being simply another enquiry into the potential for human power.

These days there is still a playful amateur interest in applying pedal-power to four wheels, with self-made multi-seat pedal-vehicles turning up at public events, often as a parody of our obsession with motor cars.

2 » Breakthrough

Industrialisation made mankind organise for bigness. Machines such as trains needed national co-ordination and infrastructure. However, another aspect of the human spirit flourished almost unnoticed in the far-off forests of southern Germany, a country almost untouched by the industrial revolution. In 1814 Baron von Drais, social misfit and inventor extraordinaire, took a bicycle to work. He was Master of the Forests, and used his 'running machine' for tours of inspection and for fast journeys from town to town. His breakthrough lay in recognising that a single steerable front wheel made balance possible. Pedals were not on his agenda: the rider pressed feet against the ground. Drais tried to commercialise his invention, had only limited success, and died in poverty.

3 » Pedals take off

4 » Wheels go high

5 » What a difference a chain makes

long came the pedal, and feet left the ground. The velocipede, or boneshaker as it was later called, had wooden wheels with iron tyres and a frame of wrought iron. The rider would sit cradled in the saddle, with his weight on the pelvic bones rather than on the crotch as was the case with the hobby-horse. Front-wheel drive had the obvious downside that the rider had to steer and power the same front wheel. Almost as much effort was put into steering it as into pedalling. They were also heavy – sixty pounds would be a fairly lightweight. However, the boneshaker was an important step in the development of cycling, which was on the cusp of industrialisation.

ixed front-wheel drive meant that each revolution of the pedals took the rider the same distance down the road as the circumference of the wheel. So the front wheel became as big as the rider's leg length would allow. High bicycles, later to be known as penny farthings, were reaching the peak of refinement in the mid-1880s. Direct drive, a minimal backbone and solid rubber tyres made bicycles elegantly simple, and the large tension-spoked wheel gave a more comfortable ride over rough roads. The high bicycle, the fastest vehicle on the road, was never safe. Hit a rock and you could fly over the top. It appealed to athletic and adventurous clubmen, largely from the middle classes.

icycle technology helped shape society, and was shaped by it. Nothing seemed impossible, as the power and cleverness of industrial processes were applied to machines which might revolutionise the leisure and work of millions. The idea of running a chain to the rear wheel allowed gearing to happen, which, in turn, brought about the end of the enormous front wheel. Pneumatic tyres meant real comfort, and a rollercoaster of inventiveness brought ideas of such useful and charming variety that they are almost all with us still, in modern guises.

6 » Three wheels good

7 » Class act

8 » Imagination runs wild

Mounting three wheels was partly a question of image, of steering clear of any association with the brasher, sweaty, bugle-blowing young cads who rode the ignoble high bicycle. Some tricyclists went for three wheels simply because it seemed a safer option. You could sit inside your machine instead of perching up above a great wheel with your bottom six feet from terra firma. On rough roads tricycles lurched about, each wheel coping with a different part of the roadway. If you hit an obstruction the whole machine might flick over and cartwheel along, leaving you unable to fall free of the mangling metal – and downhill bends could be fatal if a tricyclist lost control. But tricycles were perfect machines for many, being easy to mount, generally stable, and good at carrying loads.

Pedalling became the height of fashion in the mid-1890s, as the bicycle briefly became the plaything of the rich. The crowned heads of Europe were photographed awheel in the society magazines. Bicycles were hugely expensive, and were transported to public parks by personal carriage, to be ridden sedately up and down. Riding schools sprang up in all the capitals of Western Europe, and cycling became a significant part of upper class social events. Women tended to wear white, as for tennis: it betokened innocence, and the ability to afford big laundry bills.

Variety was the leitmotif as the 1890s saw a blossoming of inventiveness. Cycle technology was pushed into an astonishing selection of shapes and sizes. Combinations of wheels, triangles and chains, built around the human body, led to many new practical applications, and not a few dead-ends. Cycles were designed for delivering heavy loads, for carrying large families, for travelling photographers, as first-response fire engines, as prisoner transport vehicles, as army equipment, and much, much more. Experimentation was part of the Zeitgeist, and nothing seemed to be too bizarre. It was a time of great optimism, with the human body still central to everything.

Over five generations have now experienced bicycles. Our forbears discovered, as we have, that 'our most perfect invention' has allowed us to travel afar, to discover and appreciate the world at a sociable pace, to pass through crowded cities, distant communities and new-found wildernesses. Harming no-one, damaging nothing.

9 » Bikes break barriers

10 » Wheels for women

11 » Perfected for performance

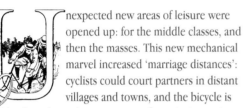nexpected new areas of leisure were opened up: for the middle classes, and then the masses. This new mechanical marvel increased 'marriage distances': cyclists could court partners in distant villages and towns, and the bicycle is said to have been the most potent factor in increasing the gene pool of humanity. The bicycle allowed millions to travel to work cheaply and independently, adding greatly to the mobility of labour. It also allowed the inhabitants of the big industrial cities to enjoy new freedoms. They could ride into the surrounding countryside at weekends, with no travel costs. The bicycle became, for many, both vehicle and symbol of a new social and political awareness.

espite bitter controversy bicycles brought independent mobility to many women, and generated social change in the areas of health, freedom of association, sexuality, clothing, rules of etiquette and cycle sport. Women were seen as the weaker sex — inferior to men by nature and culture. In 'better circles' they were always ill, pale, nervous and easily excited, and could be entrusted only with sewing, playing the piano, light housework and short promenades. It was only when women had begun to discover cycling as the source of a new lust for life that some doctors and scientists recognised that exactly these weaknesses were caused by lack of exercise, confinement to the house and low levels of mental stimulation. The bicycle was a catalyst for massive change amongst the bicycle-owning classes.

rowing fascination for the potential of pedal-power gave birth to a multitude of exciting sports. The roads and velodromes of the industrialised world witness feats of human endurance involving speeds no human had ever attained unaided. Suddenly people were racing enormous distances, requiring organisation, prizes and newspapers to sponsor and report. Tragedy and triumph enthralled the masses, celebrities were worshipped, and the keeping of records meant that sportspeople did not have to be in the same race to compete against each other. Road-racing, time-trialling and track racing were the mainstays — joined these days by mountain bike trialling, BMXing, and downhill racing. There's hardly an end to the variety of competitive cycling.

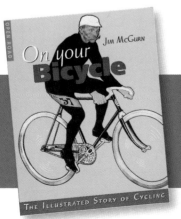

Handmade Bikes »

For a very few cycling connoisseurs only bespoke will do

David Wrath-Sharman
and his Highpath Cross Country bicycle »
Photo: Sue Darlow

Once upon a time virtually every bicycle frame on the planet was made from steel tubing. Over the years tubing for frames became lighter as stronger alloys were developed which allowed for ever thinner tube wall thicknesses. Stronger equals thinner equals lighter. Chromium, molybdenum, manganese and magnesium have all been used as alloying agents in varying amounts in the manufacture of high grade steel and are combined with careful heat-treatment processes, forging and advanced extrusion techniques. After a hundred years of such alchemy and manipulation, the steel tubing used in bike frames was approaching the end of its evolutionary development. The wall thicknesses of today's highest grades of steel frame tubes are less than 0.5mm, barely twice the thickness of a human hair. They couldn't get the tubes any thinner, so they couldn't get them any lighter.

In the quest for the lightest frame material many alternative materials have been tried – alloys of titanium, aluminium, magnesium as well as glass, aramid and carbon fibre-reinforced composites. Each has its unique properties and limitations. Many different tube construction and frame assembly techniques were investigated – casting, adhesive bonding, brazing and various types of welding. Most of these materials and technologies were dead-ends but the result of this experimentation was the eventual sidelining of steel as a high-end frame material. Aluminum, titanium and carbon-fibre composites can all be made into frames which are lighter than steel.

>> Ted James' bike for his mum, Michele
Image: Lydia Whitmore

Aluminium squeezed steel out of the middle and upper price range first, then as the sheer volume of aluminium frames coming off the production lines increased so the economics of scale drove the prices down. Factory-built titanium and the new and exotic carbon-fibre composites soon drove steel out of the high end. Inexpensive aluminum frames eventually drove steel out of most manufacturer's ranges altogether. Steel, as a bicycle frame material, had outlived its usefulness.

The last bastion of steel bicycle frames was the very bottom of the pile – the cheapest brands, the supermarket bikes. Gas pipe bikes.

Steel bikes had taken their last breath – or so it seemed… When you are a high-dollar bike geek, when you have owned and ridden the finest heat-treated scandium-alloyed aluminum, titanium, and composite monocoques where do you go next? Production bikes are great, they perform beautifully, they're fast, light, durable. The trouble is that one Brand X £5000 top-

of-the-range superbike is exactly the same as the next Brand X £5000 top-of-the-range superbike. Such is the nature of mass production.

For those who have been there and done it all the next level is bespoke, known in the trade as 'custom' or 'handmade'.

Today, the fastest growing end of the market is the Hand-Made sector. It doesn't register on the radar of most bicycle buyers because it still represents a tiny fraction of the global cycle manufacturing industry. It might be the fastest growing sector but a fast-growing tiny thing is still a tiny thing.

Throughout the decline of steel frame bikes a handful of skilled artisans remained, toiling away making steel bikes by hand. Custom, hand-built bikes never went away. Small builders have struggled over the years to compete with cycling's big manufactories. They couldn't compete on price with the big brands, they couldn't compete on frame weight with the

new generation of mass produced superbikes. Where they could outgun the competition was tailoring and options. A custom bike is measured to fit like a bespoke suit, designed to meet your exacting requirements and built to last a lifetime. If you know what you are doing you can specify tyre clearance, chain-stay length even wheel-base, but most put their trust in the experience of their chosen builder.

This resurgence in custom bikes is most welcome. It tells us that cyclists haven't forgotten what an incredibly well developed material steel is for making bike frames. It might not make the lightest frames on the planet but it builds a bike which is lively, comfortable and durable. And when a complete bike weighs in at 20 to 25 pounds what's a pound or two between friends?

The cost of a custom bike is the greatest hurdle. Prices for the very finest hand-made bikes are astonishing, particularly for folk familiar only with the other end of the market. When it comes to cars, or motorbikes, hi-fidelity, antiques or fine art some folk are happy to spend hundreds of thousands to have the very best. And no-one bats an eyelid. A bicycle might be a simple thing but you really can have the best in the world, beautiful, unique and built just for you, for not much more than an off-the shelf production bike.

And that's a bargain.

>> Square Built, Brooklyn, NY

For more information on handmade bikes visit **www.cyclorama.net/handmade**

Bilenky Cycle Works »

It was in England that American Stephen Bilenky first learned the noble trade of bicycle frame-building. He is still a bicycle Anglophile and has created a frame-building workshop in the great English tradition, offering customers design features from bikes of decades past that are rarely found on modern bikes. Bilenky's famous craftsmanship is based on nearly 50 years of experience in the bicycle business. He started in the bicycle trade in the 1960s and eventually owned a bicycle repair shop in Philadelphia PA called the Bike Doctor. In 1982 he started building custom bicycle frames in his own workshop in Phily, originally called Sterling Tandems. Bilenky Cycle Works, was founded in 1992.

Today BCW produces about 100 framesets a year, and retrofits S & S couplers (a hardware system by which frames can be taken apart for travel), repairs frames and builds forks, racks, and stems.
BCW's output ranges from show-quality beauties and stout tourers to lightweight racers out of the newest steels. BCW's aesthetic sense is as broad as its range. They make tandems, half recumbent/half upright 'viewpoint' tandems, front-racked porteurs, and freight bikes. Their tube connection techniques range from fluid fillets to purposeful TIG welds and fancy, hand-carved lugs. BCW is a frequent award winner at the annual North American Handmade Bicycle Show.

« Paulus Quiros 🇬🇧

With a team of two experienced frame builders Paulus Quiros is a pretty capable operation. However, it is not their undeniable technical skill which impresses most but the way they manipulate steel tubes and lugs to create things of such great beauty.

Though their workshop is located on the South Wales coast their designs should be seen in the context of Spain's rich artistic heritage. With a strong Art Deco influence and with hints of Gaudi, even Dali, these extraordinary bicycles wouldn't look out of place on an art gallery wall.

Norwid » ▬

Norwid are renowned for their touring, randonneur and road racing bikes made from Columbus steel and stainless-steel, as well as Reynolds 953 stainless. Frames are lugged or fillet-brazed and a particular specialty is the use of mega-size steel tubing for heavy duty riders. Norwid build bikes which are as unique as their rider, without following fashion trends. These bikes are built with years of experience and passion, and go beyond their original function. Bikes with soul. They call it their *Velosophy*.

Trollhättan pictured: »
Brushed stainless, brazed with 56% silver solder with hand-lined 'fleur-de-lys' lugs.

14 Bike Co. » 🏴󠁧󠁢󠁥󠁮󠁧󠁿

British bikes once had a reputation as being among the best in the world. 14 Bike Co was established to rekindle that spirit. Using only British Reynolds steel tubing their frames are hand-crafted without compromise by two of the best builders in the UK. Each bike is made to order, measured to fit and assembled in-house with the finest components to the client's individual requirements.

English Cycles »

Englishman-in-the-USA Rob English has a unique approach to building high performance bikes. Unusually, he still believes that iron has a place at the high performance end of the periodic table. With a background which includes an engineering degree, a very creditable TT and Human Powered Vehicle racing history and plenty of time spent working in bicycle shops — his output includes mountain bikes, road and TT bikes, kids' bikes and even a folding recumbent tandem. Plenty skilled then. But the most impressive thing about him is his ability to produce world-class, sub-15lb bikes in steel when everyone else has turned to aluminium, titanium or carbon-fibre composites. He is driven by performance. That his bikes are unfailingly and stunningly good-looking seems merely a happy by-product.

Thomas Veidt »

Thomas Veidt is a German custom builder whose speciality is making real, high quality bikes for small people. He also makes bikes for very small people. The great majority of bicycle manufacturers — whether mass-produced or low volume — simply don't make bikes for anyone who doesn't fit the 99th percentile. Which means that for most small people the choice is stark: ride a child's bike or don't ride at all. Very few children's bikes are good enough for real riding. Often it's not just about size, no children's bike can compensate for someone whose bodily proportions as well as their dimensions are outside of the 'norm'. Veidt makes it possible.

» This bike's frame size is a mere 23cm. Wheel size: 24". Total weight: 7.5 kg. Built for a rider who is 125 cm tall.

Beautiful Mover »

Bike and body together make a bio-mechanical partnership like no other. But what really happens when you get on your bike? Jim McGurn tells the story.

Put foot to pedal and the adventure of body, mind, and metal begins.

Our legs, the strongest levers we have, give life to a machine so minimal, so slight, that it's almost magical. The bicycle, only a fifth the weight of a single car wheel, takes forces equivalent to ten times its own weight. Our metabolic energy converts to kinetic energy, which ends up at the tiny point at which rear wheel rubber touches the rest of the planet. The best way to make that energy-journey, from pedal to power-point, has been worked on for nearly two centuries. Some developments, such as the transmission carry, with astonishing efficiency, virtually all the forces of the human engine through hundreds of intricate pieces of wafer-thin metal. The human bio-engine has been under development for a touch longer, and puts bicycle engineering into the primitive class.

Let's start with communication systems. Cables transmit mechanical messages to brakes and gears, but your own internal messaging systems do things differently. While you enjoy the ride, your nervous system gets on with sending, receiving, and processing billions of impulses, so that all muscles and organs can work in harmony. Your central nervous system holds the whole act together, while your peripheral nervous system does the regional work. Meanwhile your autonomic nervous system is regulating and co-ordinating vital bodily functions without you having any say in the matter. Having complete control of your bike is one thing; your own body is something else. Your mind has only partial control of a machine which co-ordinates over six hundred muscle engines, makes a thousand subtle internal adjustments a second, and runs its own continuously variable metabolism.

Nerve impulses make your muscles contract and relax, often several times a second. Two sets of opposing

muscles, made up of many fibres, give power to your limbs. One set contracts, often halving the fibres' original length. This extends the other set of muscles, time and time again.

Bones move with ease. Frame tubes are outperformed by the engineering behind your bones: a composite material, made up of carbonate crystals, giving huge compressive strength and rigidity. These carbonate crystals are bound up with collagen fibres, giving tensile strength and some flexibility. The result is a two-phase material similar to fibreglass, but vastly superior in many ways. Our technology can make things as strong as bone using aluminium or steel, but they are not as light and they don't have bone's astonishing ability to repair itself. Bone is also more elastic than steel, and so absorbs shocks better.

Wheel bearings turn in a simple bath of grease. Your body's bearings are engineered to higher levels of subtlety. The articulated joints between your bones are made up of a fibrous wall enclosing a cavity filled with fluid. Within the fibrous wall are cartilages, protecting and guiding the movement of the joint. Together with the fluid they create a movement smoother than wet ice sliding on wet ice.

Where does all the power come from? Ultimately from the sun of course: we're all solar-powered. Your immediate power-source is biochemical. While bicycle metal remains more or less inert during the ride (apart, perhaps, from some oxidisation), your muscles are powered by the energy released when a chemical bond is broken to convert ATP (adenosine triphospate) into ADP (adenosine diphosphate) and phosphate.

There's a hill ahead. The metabolic engine demands more air. Lungs fill and empty, but help is needed, so the smooth muscles surrounding them relax, for more efficient breathing. You suddenly turn up the power, drawing on the most immediate supply of ATP – that which is easily accessible in the muscles themselves. Up to ten seconds of instant, unquestioning energy, and very useful in panic situations. Your body has other tricks, too. A further quick chemical reaction can reform some of the ATP and boost this to about 30 seconds of instant energy. This reserve is gradually replenished by any ATP produced from other means and not used immediately.

The hill becomes meaner, and all the easy-access ATP runs out. You call on a second system for producing the stuff: glycolysis. This involves the breakdown of glycogen by the liver, which releases it as glucose into the bloodstream, sending a burst of energy to your legs. Other glucose is summoned from storage in muscle glycogen. It needs a chain of reactions and so takes more time, but it can give you a large amount of APT at a high rate.

This chemical reaction has a drawback well known to cyclists: it produces lactate, which builds up in the muscle fibres, causing cramps and a burning feeling in tired muscles. The aerobic energy system, which has been ticking over nicely on the flat, is unable to cope by itself. Years of cycling have given you a high tolerance to lactate, but your nervous system is reporting pain messages. Can the hill be climbed before the lactate builds up too much?

The human motor loses efficiency, while some of the body's systems are diverted to removing lactate from the muscles. It's eventually transported to the liver, and later reformed into glucose, using ATP created in yet another way.

This third way of generating ATP is aerobic – based on the use of oxygen. It's the slowest, but it's also the one that brings long-term stability. It involves a more complicated chain of chemical reactions than anaerobic glycolysis, and can call on either glucose/glycogen or stored body fat for energy. The aerobic process can produce ATP at a continuous rate without build-up of significant waste products. This is the bio-technology most used by experienced long-distance cyclists.

The aerobic reactions take place in the mitochondria inside your cells, rather than at the point at which the ATP is used. This is more efficient in terms of production, but means that the system's reaction time is slowed still further. This transition from short-term to long-term metabolism is the sudden feeling of actually getting going which cyclists recognise early in the ride.

Your riding pal overtakes, and it becomes a race to the top. Excitement messages flash across a zillion neurons, and adrenaline, nature's fast-working additive, is released into your bloodstream. The extra power is found, in a neat

and efficient way. Just enough when you need it.

Going downhill, you have the experience to keep your legs spinning, to help the blood flow and flush out the lactate. The power-demand may be over, but the liver is still busy. It is still using aerobic ATP to deal with lactate. This is one of the main reasons why you remain breathless for a while after a piece of serious cycling.

With no big load on your muscle or energy systems the aerobic ATP production can start to restock your muscles, where blood glucose can be stored as glycogen ready for the next big push. All the time the liver continues to release its stored glycogen as blood glucose.

All the while your digestive system is busy. It takes a while for food energy to get into the bloodstream, but your regular snacks have kept everything in balance, including the supply of glucose to the liver and muscles via the blood, and of water and salt, to replace lost sweat.

The terrain flattens out, and you hit a good rhythm. Adrenaline begins to wear off, but your lungs and heart have adjusted to the heavier demand and will continue at this rate. Provided the fitness and nutrition are there, your body can keep this up all day, and day after day. Those

famous 1760 kilometres on the energy equivalent of a gallon of petrol.

Your heart rate can rise and fall with ease. Yours is a cyclist's heart, used to quick action and demanding service. It pumps up the blood pressure, pushing oxygen and nutrients throughout your system. This process is helped by your warmed up muscles, as more blood surges through the capillaries, at the extremities of the bloodstream. The fuel needs to be everywhere fast. At the same time, carbon dioxide and other materials produced by the cells must be picked up for removal from your body. This is the task of your circulatory system. The exchange of oxygen and carbon dioxide between blood and body cells takes place in the network of tiny capillaries, blood vessels a single cell thick, just under the skin, You carry round over 60,000 miles (100,000 km) of blood vessels.

Your muscles are throwing out heat. This is also carried through the blood into the capillaries, causing glands on your skin to secrete sweat. This evaporates, cooling the surrounding skin and also the blood in the capillaries. Your sweat itself is not hot, and it doesn't carry heat away directly.

At the end of the ride you allow your body to wind down slowly. The metabolic increase can last for several hours yet, digesting food and reordering the reserves of energy around your body, like a train marshalling yard. Moving all the lactate and other fatigue poisons from the various muscles to your liver takes time, and your body remains at a higher level of activity until much of this is done. Recharging the glycogen stores in your liver and muscles is also done, ready for the next ride.

A bike is a pretty piece of nothing until you give it a reason for being. Put your foot on that pedal and you become the most elegant and efficient mover in the entire known universe.

"No bicycle can match the mechanics of the human body, but together they reach new heights of efficiency and potential, making the perfect partnership. The physics of the bike are now well known, but the bio-physics of our bodies are still being understood."

Fundamentals of Fit »

Even with the finest frame and components you'll be going nowhere fast if your bike doesn't fit you properly. Mick Allan advises on how to make the perfect match.

To make life easy for the folk who manufacture bicycles human beings were long ago standardised. We don't come in a huge range of sizes and it's possible to make quite broad generalisations about the ratio of our limbs to our torso. It's why 99% of the population can walk into any bike shop and find a bike to suit them right off the shop floor.

Why then are so many people riding bikes which are poorly adjusted or worse – entirely the wrong size? We have no trouble buying shoes to fit so why are bicycles so difficult? Bikes are available in a range of sizes. Cheap bikes from mail-order catalogues and supermarkets might come in only one or two sizes. At the other end of the scale custom builders will measure every major bone in your body before brazing together the perfect bike just for you. The kind you'll find in your local bike store, come in three to five sizes. They're also a bit gender specific – more on that later.

These 'frame sizes' always refer to the nominal length of the seat tube (from the centre of the bottom bracket, where the cranks rotate, to the top of the seat tube where the seat goes in). You'll hear numbers like 'seventeen and a half inches' or 'fifty-eight centimetres'.

So far so good. But now it gets silly. As anyone who sells bikes for a living will tell you, the length of the seat-tube is actually kind of irrelevant. What we are really interested in is what's known as reach. Reach is the distance from the seat to the handlebar. You are probably aware that it's possible to raise or lower the seat on most bikes: anything

up to eight inches on some. But what you can't do is significantly alter the reach. Which means you have to get it right. In addition, and just to confuse us even more, the seat-tube length to reach ratio varies between brands, models and even frame sizes. Don't get fitted to a 52cm Brand X and assume that a 52cm Brand Y will fit you too.

When we are sizing a bike for someone we start by establishing their *minimum stand-over clearance*. It is essential that there is a decent gap between the underneath of you and the top-tube. Simply stand astride the bike with your feet flat on the floor, then grab the stem with one hand and the saddle with the other and lift the bike up as high as it will go. Gently..! Try and keep it level and ask someone to measure how much of a gap you have under your wheels. On a street bike, racer or touring bike this might be as little as an inch (25mm); on a mountain bike we aim for no less than four inches (100mm). This procedure establishes the largest frame size a person can safely ride in that particular model.

At this stage we adjust the saddle to suit the inside leg dimension of the rider. Technically we are starting with the lower pedal as our datum and adjusting the saddle in relation to it. That's the saddle height. It's a given. Fore and aft adjustment of the saddle is determined by the length of the rider's femur. We aim to have the back of the rider's knee cap directly above the pedal spindle when the pedal is at its furthest forward position. So using a couple of tools and a piece of string, within a few minutes we can have an individual's saddle to within a very few mms of perfect.

If you're trying out a new city or street bike it's likely that the handlebars will already be in pretty much the right position. Nevertheless there is usually some adjustability available: up, down, fore, aft and rotate. If you feel the urge you may fine-tune your position to the nth degree using just an Allen key or two. And it's worth doing. Spend a little time getting the set-up just right, even adjusting the position of the brake and shift levers, and your cycling miles will be so much more comfortable. Most people don't. Because they don't know how? Because they haven't the tools? Can't be bothered? I don't know for sure. I suspect that most people just don't know what a well fitted bike is supposed to feel like. So they contort their bodies and spend their days riding with the saddle too low and the bars too far away.

On mid to high end bikes the universal adoption of the 'threadless' headset system means that handlebar stem adjustment is limited or even impossible. Relocating the handlebar is a matter of swapping out the stem for one with a different length or rise.

Vital Statistics...

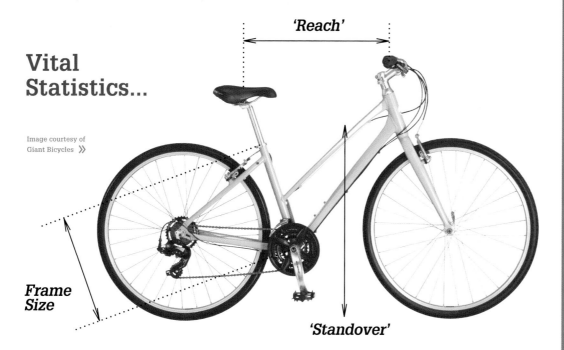

Image courtesy of
Giant Bicycles »

'Reach'

**Frame
Size**

'Standover'

Considering that women make up more than half of the population it's taken a shockingly long time for manufacturers to get their collective mind around the idea that women might like to ride decent bikes, too.

Women's saddles are slightly shorter and slightly wider than men's saddles. This is because women have shallower pelvises and their *ishial tuberosities* (butt bones) are slightly further apart. It is quite impossible for a normal woman to feel comfortable on a man's saddle. For some the experience will put them off cycling forever because a skinny saddle sits up in between the sit bones and body weight is carried entirely by the soft tissue. Ouch.

Women's bikes come in two forms: ladies' bikes, (more correctly referred to as 'open', 'loop' or 'low step-through') and women's specific – that is regular looking, bikes with a top-tube which have been designed to fit the unique proportions of the female form. You see (generalisation alert!) a woman will have longer legs than a man of the same height. Women also have smaller hands and shorter arms and, most significantly, those differently shaped

pelvises. As a result women require shorter top tubes or less reach. And this is the key difference between bikes designed for men and women.

It is possible to fit your average woman on to a regular ('gent's') bike. Before women-specific bikes were available it was simply a case of fitting a women's saddle, speccing a slightly smaller frame and possibly a shorter stem to compensate. Women-specific bikes are absolutely a step in the right direction but if you are not a particularly small woman the option of installing a women's saddle on a regular ('man's') bike is a perfectly acceptable solution and will give you more model options. You just need to be fitted by someone who knows what they are doing.

Loop frames on the other hand are ideal for anyone, male or female, with limited mobility or who just want to be able to get off the bike quickly, such as in heavy traffic. Also, if you have a kid's seat on the back then a low step-through allows you to mount your bike much more gracefully and without clobbering your progeny with your foot.

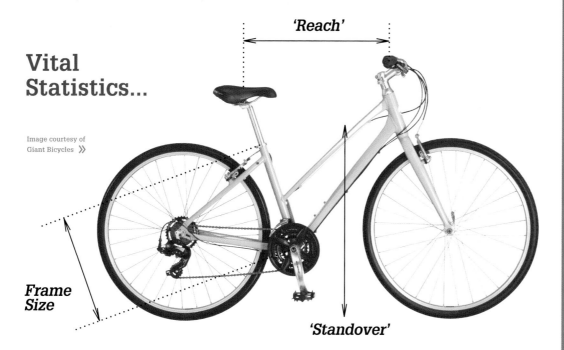

Watch out for:

▪ Handlebars, brake and gear levers are not set in stone. It's all just nuts and bolts, so you can adjust them to suit the angle of your wrists and your own personal preference. Brake levers on flat or riser bars should be in line with your arms when you are sitting on the bike. You can always move them back...

▪ Only a level saddle can support your weight effectively. A saddle which slopes up at the nose applies excess pressure to soft tissue and forces the pelvis to rotate backwards in an effort to get some weight on the sit bones and also makes the bars seem too far away. The rider cannot push hard on the pedals for fear of sliding off the back of the saddle. Conversely, a saddle which slopes down causes the pelvis to constantly slip off the front. To compensate the rider must constantly push their body weight back up off the bars and pedals. This set-up failure encourages the use of unduly high gears and, again, because so much weight has been transferred to the bars they feel way too low. It's really easy to mess up an otherwise perfectly good set-up just by having the saddle a couple of degrees out. As a general rule the more upright the riding position the wider the saddle should be.

▪ Contrary to expectations firm saddles are more comfortable than squishy ones. It's because a firm saddle is better able to support your body weight.

▪ If your saddle is doing its job properly it should never enter your thoughts. The same can be said about the whole bike. For extreme long-distance cycling comfort is all important – but the same ergonomic principles apply to whatever bike you ride.

Fixed »

Fixed-wheel, or fixed-gear, riding is as close as you will get to perpetual motion. It's cycling at its purest.

» Heritage, Paris

» Marin Dominican

» Poppy's Bike from Ted James

» Herne Hill

Freewheels are so common that we hardly notice their existence. Until recently the freewheel-free bicycle was the preserve of a small band of hardened souls – track racers and winter road riders. Speak to a fixed-wheel rider about why they ride fixed and they'll struggle to find the words. They'll talk of feeling 'more connected' with their machine. They might even use words and phrases like 'pure' and 'at one', and they'll be frustrated that words alone can't ever really explain what riding fixed feels like. One of the much quoted benefits is that fixed-wheel bicycles have fewer moving parts than multi-speed bikes and so require less maintenance. But no one ever rode a fixed just because it was easier to maintain.

On a bicycle the freewheel is a component within the transmission incorporating a series of ratchets which allows drivetrain 'over-run'. In other words it allows the pedaller to stop pedalling while the machine is in motion. In years gone by a few high-end car manufacturers used them to disengage the engine from the drive wheels, notably Rolls-Royce and Cord, whose customers demanded quieter transmissions.

A freewheel can be thought of as an automatic clutch which allows your legs to turn slower than the driven wheel. It's the bit which makes the ticking noise when you are coasting down a hill. Because it 'unlocks' the pedals from the drivetrain a freewheel mechanism makes a bike easier to use, it allows for multi-speed derailleur gear systems and lets us corner safer/harder/faster because we can raise the inside pedal to stop it striking the ground.

The earliest – front wheel drive – pedal-powered machines were 'fixed', all the way up to the high-wheeled penny farthings. So too were the very first chain-drive 'safeties'. Ernst Sachs (the soul of whose company still lives on in the SRAM Corporation) was the first to produce freewheels in commercial quantities in 1898. Though William van Anden had patented the freewheel many years earlier in 1868 it wasn't until the widespread adoption of the safety bicycle with its chain and sprockets that it really came into its own.

Hop on the saddle and the first thing you notice is the difficulty of getting your feet on the pedals when the cranks cannot be spun backwards. It feels broken. Underway the first few timid turns of the pedal feel OK. You pedal. It moves. You trundle around. Just like a regular bike… And then, just when you thought everything was under control, comes the first dawning of just what you've let yourself in for – when, just for a fraction of a second, you stop pedalling. The very last thing you want to do on a fixed-wheel is stop pedalling. The momentum of your bodyweight is still driving that back wheel around, which continues to feed the chain over the sprocket, which drives the cranks and promptly gives you an almighty kick through the pedals. The very least that happens at this point is a kind of primordial shiver up the spine.

Riding fixed is certainly more difficult. It demands 100% concentration and total respect, because if you're hurtling along and forget – even for a moment – to keep your legs turning a fixed-wheel will dash you to the ground in the blink of an eye. Catch a pedal in a corner and you'll be hurled in the air. Fixed knows no mercy.

But all this talk of pain and suffering hides a truth – there is nothing like riding fixed.

If the bike is moving so are your legs. This allows you to control speed, and even stop completely, without using the brakes. It's easy to make subtle changes of speed and pace according to the conditions and it is partly this connectedness with the rear wheel which made fixed-wheel bikes popular winter hacks. Fixed riders can feel the tyre contact point in a way

freewheel equipped riders cannot and in slippery or icy conditions this ability to feel the limit of traction can make the difference between road-rash and staying in the saddle. In practice (and, in many territories, in law) this ability to brake the rear wheel through back pressure on the pedals means that a fixedwheel bike built for the road may dispense with the rear caliper and run only a front brake. Though it has something of a hard-core cult following, riding fixed with no front brake is a step too far for most – outside of a velodrome.

As you cycle along your momentum propels the pedals over the dead spot. There is no derailleur tension, there are no jockey wheels, no superfluous chain and no extra sprockets and rings to haul around so bike weight and transmission drag is minimised. There is only one gear and its ratio is determined by the relationship of the chainring to the sprocket multiplied by the size of the rear wheel. The ratio must be chosen carefully on the basis of the steepness of the local terrain. Bikes in hilly cities have different ratios from those in flatter areas. A bike must be geared just low enough to get up the steepest hill around without popping a patella, but this needs to be traded against the challenge of descending the same hill. Downhill – legs must spin like an egg-whisk or you risk losing control. Fixed encourages high revs over high torque and this, combined with the constant pedalling, promotes excellent cardiovascular fitness. To go faster you cannot shift up a gear, the only option, the only option, is to pedal faster.

But when you 'get' it – When you have enough mileage in your legs to make them strong and lean and supple. When you can rush that hill like a March hare and, over the top, spin out down the other side at 150+rpm without missing a beat... When you can trackstand until the cows come home without dabbing a foot... When you get it, there is no experience like it in the world.

Fixed Wheel Freestyle

A couple of years ago, virtually overnight, everyone and their sibling took to riding around on fixed wheels. Inevitably some of them began fooling around on them. Street BMX riding requires an unusually high level of skill, but doing stunts on a regular fixedwheel bike is another kettle of fish altogether. Skids is one thing, but grinding street furniture is asking for trouble. And, even if the humans were up to the job, the skinny-assed track bikes they were abusing were definitely not. And so the people who breed bicycles herded two of them up, threw them together in a field and we politely averted our gaze as rough-and-ready street BMX got jiggy with refined and elegant track bike. The snarling mongrels which emerged from the sordid encounter looked like track bikes in suits of BMX chromoly armour. You'd have to be a loony to ride one.

For more information on fixed wheel bikes visit **www.cyclorama.net/fixed**

« Sexy Bicycles Pulse
by Flying Machine

Flying Machine is a bicycle design studio that produces distinctive, superlative quality bicycles for individuals and business customers worldwide. Comprising Sexy Bicycles, Base Urban and Special Projects, the bikes are designed in Western Australia using custom-made components and strikingly fresh, high quality finishes. *Sexy Bicycles* offer exclusivity through limited production volumes, high-design aesthetic and superior quality construction.

Base Urban provides a range of bicycles perfectly suited to the rigours of urban life. Low maintenance, ease of operation, consistent performance and durability are key developments with a distinctly minimal aesthetic.

Special Projects designs and produces custom bicycles for a wide range of business purposes.

Unique to Flying machine's model is the ability to produce as few as twenty bikes per order, enabling even small cycle businesses to secure exceptional custom-branded bicycles. Large-quantity orders are given an equal standard of bespoke design and performance. Bicycles coming out of Flying Machine's studio embody the simplicity of form and function which comes from real creativity and care with detail.

The bike shown above, the Sexy Bicycles Pulse, is a Limited Production fixed wheel bike which features a monocoque carbon fibre frame and fork, hand-built carbon wheel set, adorned with some of the finest components available and finished in exquisite high quality 'liquid' paint.

Sexy Bicycles Fresh
Sexy Bicycles Heat 1 Speed
Base Urban FX-2.0

« The Viktor ▬
by Schindelhauer

Schindelhauer have taken the traditional fixed-wheel bike and introduced it to the future. The Viktor is one of a range of exquisitely detailed machines which use cutting edge technology to deliver high levels of performance and durability — all wrapped up in a cleanly designed and superbly detailed package. Stand-out details include concealed headset and clean running Gates Carbon belt drive.

DF3 Trackbike »
by Dolan 🇬🇧

UCI rules dictate that track bikes must be fixed-wheel and brakeless. They are also massively stiff and brutally fast. Running super-high-pressure glue-on 'tubular' tyres on bladed or disc wheels they are simultaneously hard-as-nails and too delicate for anything but the smoothest of wooden (indoor) or concrete (outdoor) banked track surfaces. Even here there are a range of different specialist machines for different disciplines, from exhilarating break-neck sprints to the daunting, and lonely 'hour'.

The New Rich »

Robert Poole

» Photo: Robin Thom

Every age has its new rich – traditionally those who have in one or two generations managed to acquire wealth but not culture. They are often seen as showy, social climbers, all fur coat and no finesse. They mistake the sign (money) for the thing (value). They simulate taste by buying ornaments, and popularity by buying friends. They live by conspicuous consumption – waste by any other name.

Times are changing. Waste is out, sustainability is in. In the age of affluence, economy is conspicuous; in the age of cheap dyes, black and white is sophisticated; in an age of noise, silence is precious. Who are the new rich now? Consider my friend Sarah. She lives and works in a medium-sized town. She doesn't run a car, but cycles instead, most of her journeys being local. If she wants to go further, the main-line railway station is nearby. If she wants to carry loads or infirm friends, she has a fleet of vehicles at her disposal, 24 hours a day: the taxi system. Sarah has no car, but she is highly mobile. But she doesn't need to travel a lot: she has chosen her place and put down roots.

Not running a car saves her money – a lot of money. With the money saved Sarah can make all the journeys she needs: by bike, taxi, train, bus, folding bike, even hire car, and have change left over to buy a new bike every year. She has money left over to buy (should she wish) all the books she has time to read, all the music she has time to listen to, and all the meals out she has time to eat. Not only that, but not being a car driver she doesn't get landed with all those tasks at work that involve hammering up and down motorways and getting stuck in traffic jams. And of course she doesn't need a house with a garage.

Not running a car saves Sarah something more valuable than money: time. Sarah's lifestyle means she lives near her work, so she spends perhaps twenty minutes a day commuting rather than the more typical hour or two. She doesn't have to work to pay for the car she hasn't got. All those meals out mean she doesn't have to spend much time cooking, or run a kitchen full of gadgets and stale ingredients.

Then there is the lifestyle factor that comes from cycling. Every cyclist knows about that; in Sarah's case it is symbolised by the daily ride to work through a park with a magnificent view over the bay while colleagues fume amongst the traffic far below. Their transport is their stress; her cycle is her therapy. Recently Sarah learnt that regular cyclists are medically ten years younger than non-cyclists. Having just passed 40, she realised there was no point in waiting until retirement age to cash in those ten years. She decided to have her thirties all over again, and thanks to good health and optimism she may just get away with it, for a while anyway.

Sarah is one of the new new rich – rich, that is, in terms of lifestyle rather than money. On a slightly above-average income, she wants for nothing serious, and is able to afford anything within reason that she has time for. She is rich, in both time and resources, precisely because she does not have to spend one-fifth of her waking life either driving a car or working to pay for it.

Sarah is a model economic unit. Successful businesses these days carry as little surplus capital and stock as they can, preferring to buy in services from others as and when needed. The typical successful shop has a limited stock, well-selected and displayed, and a rapid turnover.

It runs with a minimum of staff, hiring fitters, cleaners, couriers, vans and so on as needed. It is brisk, light and efficient.

So is Sarah. She does well because she doesn't carry a lot of capital – the car, and all the social gubbins that goes with it. With what she saves, she can (indirectly) hire the labour of others to feed her, transport her, mend her clothes and her bikes, deliver her groceries. She doesn't register very highly on the national income balance sheet, but in terms of resources at her disposal and quality of life, Sarah is an economic miracle compared with those of her colleagues who struggle to touch their toes on twice the income.

Much of Sarah may be recognisable in you. Her life has the same sort of problems as anyone else's, but she's probably lean and flexible enough to cope. If things go wrong she can afford a break from work.
So: are you one of the new rich? Cyclists tend to be hostile to conventional economics, and with good reason: it ignores social costs, and can't count non-material benefits. But with a little imagination you can put a price of sorts on the beneficial spin-offs of being a cyclist. It has been well said that the truly wealthy are those who know how to count their blessings.
It can be a cheering exercise to compute the benefits of being a cyclist: try applying the calculation to your own life some time.

> ❝ In a wasteful, high-stress age when the benefits of 'downshifting' are enviable, the cyclist (if you'll pardon the pun) is the original downshifter. ❞

Psycholists »

Are we a neurotic bunch of social outcasts, or well-balanced individuals at peace with our mode of transport?

» Woodcut: David Eccles

What's psychology got to do with cycling? Does everything really have to be deconstructed and analysed – isn't it enough to know that cycling's a pleasant and efficient way to travel? And what's the end result of this analysis going to be? That cyclists are generally neurotic, have some sort of anti-car fixation, or are psychosomatically indisposed to sit inside metal boxes?

Behind the everyday facade of triviality are complete worlds and counterworlds, hidden promises, assumptions and beautiful solutions to the paradoxical problems of our mental lives. In cycling, we are involved in a spiritual journey, so much more than just a journey from A to B. It is a playful way to turn the world on its head, to break through conventional boundaries and to reassess modern day behaviour. The bicycle represents a return to a childlike simplicity. It puts reality into the mantra that less is more.

But cycling is also a sort of polemic. It is fun, but it provokes. It is easy, yet requires exertion. It is banal and trivial, yet it's an artistic expression of motion. It is a step backwards and a step to progress.

These paradoxes extend to cyclists, too. They're often both more cranky yet somehow more human than many of their car-loving contemporaries. When they cycle they

This is an edited extract from 'It's those Cyclists again! – a Short Psychology of Cycling', by Michael Degen. Translation is by Jim McGurn. Immer diese Radfahrer – kleine Psychologie des Radfahrens, Rasch und Röhring, ISBN 3-89136-207-2.

are being sensible and yet are imaginatively comical. On the streets they are victim and culprit in one. They are artists of the everyday, and cycling is their everyday artistic creation.

Cycling belongs to a class of 'simple things' which we seek out when we need to relax. Like sex, you don't have to think about it too much. You just give yourself over to it, it moves along happily, it satisfies. It pretty much happens automatically. Simple.

As with sexual relationships, difficulties and conflicts are never far away. Cycling is only simple at a 'basic' level. Cycling is one of those 'simple things' which is much more complicated in adult life than in childhood. It implies an idealisation of childhood. The ways of adulthood in contrast are too burdensome, too complex. Almost every cyclist has fond memories of the bicycle as part of their childhood, associated with new adventures, with empowerment and new skills. The bicycle stands for successful learning. For the discovery of new worlds.

Grown-ups often portray a child's view of the world as direct and unfiltered, easy and rich in experience. Those who rediscover cycling as adults often want to relive this ideal of childhood – to be free from adult inhibitions, and to seek a new form of originality.

The Hats We Wear »

» The Posers

The level of their equipment is out of all proportion to their actual performance. They always want the latest and the best. But it's rather like owning a top-quality sound system and only playing Barry Manilow. Posers have no idea how to use their gear properly. They just get a kick out of owning it. ~ *Full Carbon Multi-vent Aero*

» The Sports Cyclists

They treat cycling as hard work. They are members of a cycling club, ride a hell of a lot, and take part in real races. Cycling is practically their calling, and sometimes their livelihood. And their gear is generally proportional to their performance. They know what they want, and they don't waste time. ~ *Regular Helmet*

» The Fairweather Cyclists

The fair-weather cyclist's bike lives in the shed most of the time, which is why it still looks new after two years. It may be taken out for a gentle Sunday pootle, when the sun is shining, the way other people go boating on the lake. It doesn't matter if it isn't too sturdy, or develops a grinding bottom bracket after a while. Expectations are low, distances are short, and the bike will not be pushed to the limits. ~ *Alice Band*

» The Commuters

These people rely totally on their bikes. They cycle to work, to university or to do the shopping. They like bike paths, but aren't scared of the urban road: starting their pupation by riding in the gutter, but soon moving on to the art of confident and unambiguous road riding. Commuter cyclists are the free spirits of the city, but not averse to indignation when car drivers cross the invisible line which separates the wicked from the worthy. ~ *Hard Shell Skate Helmet*

» The Friends of the Fixed wheel

These people rely totally on their bikes. They cycle to work, to university or to do the shopping. They like bike paths, but aren't scared of the urban road: starting their pupation by riding in the gutter, but soon moving on to the art of confident and unambiguous road riding. Commuter cyclists are the free spirits of the city, but not averse to indignation when car drivers cross the invisible line which separates the wicked from the worthy. ~ *Vintage Italian Casquette*

» The Ideologists

These are folks of all ages who have stepped out of car culture, and can use the bicycle as a political argument. They know all the research on road traffic, and never tire of reminding everyone of how the bike is the quickest beast in town. Like the Posers, the Ideologists value performance. But they view it differently: they want to prove that cars are obsolete, and that one can do anything by bike. For ideological reasons, they don't ride a flash racer, but an old Dutch roadster, plastered with stickers reading 'For a Cleaner Future' and the like. And like the Posers, they put a tremendous amount of money into their bike. But their money is spent on extras for the Dutch roadster, such as accessories and custom-made parts – special bottom bracket, special gear shifts, leather saddle etc . The likeable thing about the Ideologists, is that they practise what they preach. They cycle in all weathers. True Ideologists never drive cars, and indeed some of them even refuse to learn how to drive. ~ *Woolly Bobble Hat*

Bike People »

It takes all sorts to cycle. Here, from around the world, are simply some people and their bikes

Clockwise from top left »
Connie Hedegaard, Danish Minister of the Environment, out for a Sunday bike ride through Copenhagen. Photo: Mikael Colville-Andersen. Rahsaan Bahati. US Pro rider and founder of bahatifoundation.org. Dave Halliday, cycling consultant and Scotsman, on a bike custom-made for his height. Neil Stanford, cycle mechanic in York, with his daughter on a Taga.

Clockwise from top left »

Performing a non-footed backflip is Jakub Kalida of the United Merida Freeriders.

Belinda and Paul from York, England, at their wedding, where all wore fancy dress. Belinda is disabled, and uses a detachable wheelchair which fits to the side of the bike Paul rides.

African Boys on bikes (Tanzania)

Enjoying hard court bike polo on a fixed wheel is Hungarian Eniko Magda.

Riding his own-make Ratcatcher is cycle designer Mike Burrows of Norwich, England, author of Bicycle Design.

Kalle Kalkhoff, maker of Pedersen Cycles in Germany, piloting his own-make tandem, with daughter Lisa as stoker.

Street Bikes »

Street Bikes, City Bikes, Town Bikes - whatever you like to call them - are purpose built for urban tarmac.

Naples »

Copenhagen »

Towns and cities are cycling's home turf. The vast majority of all journeys are less than eight kilometres (five miles) and the humble bicycle is the most efficient, inexpensive, flexible and sociable mode of transport we have. In many towns and cities it's the fastest too.

City cycling is inexpensive but that doesn't mean that a city bike should be cheap. People often mistakenly assume that a commuting bike should be from the lower end of the market (it's hard to sell decent bikes in societies where most of the population thinks that a bicycle cost less than a tank of petrol). Some folk will ride a series of horrid bikes from the catalogue or supermarket for many years and wonder why they fail so regularly. It's unrealistic to expect a super cheap bike to be pleasant to ride, comfortable and reliable – cost cutting at the factory leaves the absolute minimum required to qualify as a functioning bike. The very worst examples are barely capable of being maintained and kept on the road. The truth is, a bike which will be used every day of its life will quickly wear out or fall apart if assembled from the cheapest components. It's no surprise that so many new cycle commuters give up so soon.

There's cheap, and then there's plain wrong. Almost any kind of bike can be pressed in to service as a city bike but many styles are far from ideal. In some countries the narrowly competitive nature of the mainstream cycle industry has led to many people being sold bikes with components and features which render them quite unsuitable for the job – a kind of parallel universe where essential all-season commuting components such as mudguards and lights are presented as being 'optional extras'. It's not uncommon to see commuters bouncing along on heavy and inefficient full suspension, riding fragile racing wheels or slow knobbly off-road tyres, or using gears designed for grinding up muddy mountains or road racing down them. For urban cycling there's no point paying for handfuls of gears you'll never use, or for suspension which serves no useful purpose except another something to wear out. Unnecessary features add complexity and cost to a bike's purchase price and throughout its life at maintenance time.

A street bike is designed to be surefooted and comfortable, robust and durable. It should be capable of delivering you to your destination day-in and day-out without busting the budget in servicing. It may not be the fastest bike on the road but it will be quietly efficient, easy to pedal, and simple in operation. Gears will be slick and reliable, brakes powerful and immune to weather.

City cyclists need to arrive at their destination in the same condition as if they had come by car or by bus, which means, in many climates, mudguards, chain-guards and skirt-guards. They will to want to carry a few personal items, perhaps even a week's shopping, and to do so they need luggage racks or handlebar-mounted baskets. Lights should be bright and reliable, possibly dynamo powered and integrated into the design.

The higher the quality of the bike the more durable it will be and the more pleasant to ride, but it doesn't have to be new. A used bike may do the job perfectly well and give years of service if well maintained. It doesn't need to be super-light with all the bells and whistles and it doesn't have to cost the earth but it does need to be up to the job of day in day out riding in all weather conditions.

Because a city bike is above all a tool, and like a well used tool a city bike will get knocked about. It is not a precious object – the bangs and scrapes of city life won't faze it. Those scratches from the parking rack? The dent in the top tube from dropping it against a wall? That's life.

Every street bike is one less car on the road. Every city cyclist is a reduction in traffic congestion, pollution and a population's levels of obesity and heart disease. The growth in the market for city bikes puts inexpensive, practical, door-to-door, green, healthy and enjoyable transport at everyone's disposal.

Buy a good one.

And ride the hell out of it.

» Münster

» York

» London

Copenhagen
by Biomega » 🇩🇰

Danish company Biomega take a unique approach to creating their bikes. By employing industrial designers from outside of the bicycle industry they introduce fresh ideas and new thinking. Penned by designer Jens Martin Skibsted, the Copenhagen is the first internationally available shaft-drive bicycle. Traditional bicycle drive chains are wonderfully efficient when new and clean but soon deteriorate with exposure to the elements and a lack of care. What the shaft-drive transmission loses in ultimate efficiency is more than made up for in maintenance-free peace of mind. It's perfect technology for an every-day street bike.

With an elegantly finished frame, internally routed cables and performance oriented geometry the Copenhagen combines a sporty profile with a clean and minimalist look.

The other bikes in their range are no less innovative.

The Biomega Puma. Designed Jens Martin Skibsted the Puma features an integrated lock which is a structural part of the frame. This machine is on permanent display at the San Francisco Museum of Modern Art. »

Penned by internationally renowned product designer Marc Newson, the specially formed aluminum frame components of the MN are joined together using a bonding process which was developed for the Lotus Elise sports car. »

The Brooklyn. There's nothing practical about this town hopper! You can take this bike from your usual city playground to a sand-dune or a heap of snow without losing momentum. Made for keeping it fun no matter how harsh the terrain. »

VANMOOF
No. 3 »

Starting with a blank piece of paper VANMOOF went back to first principles. An aluminium frame delivers low weight, a coaster brake and integrated lights: practicality. The durable anodized finish means it'll still look good after years of use and abuse and its simplicity means there's very little that can go wrong. In the best traditions of modern industrial design engineering 'form follows function' and the result is a stylish, honest interpretation of a traditional European urban bike.

The entry model comes with that iconic top-tube or as a step-through and there's a version with an integrated lock. And all can be upgraded to 'Over the Top' spec which adds a front hub brake and seven internal gears.

Montego Bikes »

Urban Daily »

In places where cycling isn't a 'lifestyle choice' led by sport, but an everyday activity, manufacturers take a different approach. No great emphasis is placed on flashy graphics and the seemingly endless arms race that is gear numbers. Montego's entire range is designed for urban streets, featuring modern takes on traditional Dutch styles. The Daily Urban range includes steel and aluminum frames, single and multi speeds. But they share an upright, commanding, riding position and sensible, durable components.

So it's very encouraging, if a little ironic that, in parts of the world not normally associated with utility bikes, these bikes are becoming so trendy.

Barrow »

Inspired by classic designs the Barrow can carry a good load on its integrated front rack. It was developed in collaboration with Bleijh Concepts and Design, an Amsterdam-based design studio, whose brief was to bring cargo bikes into the 21st century.

It's a process which has resulted in a very distinctive machine. Strong oversized aluminium frame tubing provides rigidity and steering precision without excess weight, whilst the high volume Schwalbe Fat Frank tires provide a comfortable and smooth ride. The high capacity rack, which is integrated with the handlebars, keeps the cargo safely in full view of the rider.

Virtue Curve, One and Six »

It's too easy to get caught up in bicycle snobbery. We would all like to be riding around on hand-crafted wonder bikes with hand cut lugs and electronic shifting. The trouble is that although super bikes might do a lot for an individual's sense of wellbeing they don't do much for cycling. One of the attractions of cycling is that it doesn't cost the earth.

Just as no-one actually needs a gold Swiss watch to tell the time, Virtue Bike from San Diego prove that you don't have to spend a fortune to get a bike which is capable, durable and stylish.

This may be just the sort of bike we need the masses awheel. With a range of options – regular or step-thru frames and the choice of single-speed or derailleur – there's a street bike in their range to suit any need. And every pocket.

Curve 6 »

Firemans Texas Cruzer »

Few bikes come close to the kerb-jumping, knock-about capabilities of BMX bikes. If only they were bigger they would be perfect tough, short-range, street bikes for grown-ups. Hand-crafted in the USA of 100% chromoly since 1998, Firemans Texas Cruzers are a natural evolution of the leading loop-tail racing cruisers of BMX racing's heyday in the 1980's. With a choice of 24", 26" and 29" wheels they are everything a big kid could want. So good they named a beer after it. Firemans No. 4 Ale is named after the Firemans Texas Cruzer, and is brewed by The Real Ale Brewing Company in Blanco, Texas.

BigBMX »

BMX bikes are loved for their toughness, being surefooted, chuckable and fun to ride. But they are something most folk expect to grow out of in their teenage years. The designer of this bike was inspired by the thousands of single-speed Dutch bikes whilst living in Amsterdam. BigBMX combines the simple get-on-and-go reliability with the bomb-proof construction of a BMX, resulting in a brilliantly efficient street bike. Winning two consecutive first place trophies in one of the UK's competitive BMX racing championships has earned this machine enormous street credibility.

The Ciao » by Foffa

Regular urban fixed-wheel bikes are fine if you're comfortable with a performance-oriented riding position. But what if you're one of the many people who prefer higher bars — and don't want to ride a heavy roadster?

The Foffa Ciao is unusual — an upright bike which combines the performance, simplicity and easy maintenance of a single-speed/fixed-wheel with the comfort and enhanced control of an upright riding position.

There are three other models available: the single speed Prima, the step-thru Grazia and Gears — their multi-speed model based around a classic lugged frame constructed with Columbus tubing.

Foffa Bikes have taken a fresh approach to the selling of bicycles. The traditional industry model was rejected in favour of their own highly customer-centred system. Foffa customers can customize their bikes at the point of ordering through an easy-to-use online Bike Builder application. Foffa Bikes make it possible to own a classic steel bike, absolutely unique and totally personalized, without paying a fortune.

Tank Cruiser by Virtue »

Far too many cyclists are riding short urban journeys on overly complicated multi-geared, sometimes even fully suspended bikes. Sledgehammers to crack nuts. The beauty of using the right tool for a job comes not from the complexity of the tool but from its rightness. A bike for local journeys, trips to school, the store, the gym or the beach. With the timeless appeal of a traditional American cantilever frame, the Tank cruiser is another of those super simple bikes which does all that it needs to do without any fancy hoohaa, and without costing a fortune.

Helmets by Nutcase »

If there's one company which has introduced color and style to helmets, it has to be Nutcase. Their superbly designed headgear has brought urban cool to this important area of cyclewear. So if you've got a gorgeous bike, you can now have beautiful Nutcase head-art to match. Now we can look great on our bikes, knowing that our grey matter is well looked after. Even better, Nutcase helmets feature an easy-adjust fitting system. Attractive, safe, easy to wear. The three things you want from a helmet. Nutcase are an important part of bike fashion for adults, but their range of children's helmets is designed to appeal to the younger market, too.

« Cinco5
by ORTRE

If we're to have any hope of persuading urban populations to abandon their current modes and start cycling we need to present them with attractive alternatives.

There are a few basic minimum requirements of a good urban utility bike: low weight, for one, to make it easy to propel around and lug up kerbs. It must be comfortable, sure-footed and be able to carry a decent load. It needs to be mechanically uncomplicated for ease of use and easy maintenance, and it must represent good value for money.

But it's not enough to merely 'tick all the boxes', in a world of design-conscious consumers bicycles need to look good too.

When the whole of the cycling industry seems determined to look backwards in time for inspiration it's refreshing to see designers pushing forwards. Conceived in Sydney Australia, the Cinco5 is designed for short trips up to five kilometres. Lightweight, nimble urban utility — we think ORTRE might be on to something.

Dawes »

Town & Country

It's difficult to classify some bikes. Where do we draw the line between leisure-oriented comfort bike and street bike? Between street bike and trekking bike? Trekking bike and tourer? It's a spectrum, and many bikes comfortably straddle different categories. A flat-handlebar-equipped touring bike, ideal for long distance riding on less than glass-smooth tarmac, also serves pretty well as an everyday commuter.

Whether you're a 'fairweather cyclist' or an urban warrior, the fact is that very many bikes are perfectly capable of doing more than one job. And if you have room for only one bike in your life, today there are more niche bikes than ever to meet your specific needs.

Dawes Cycles has been in business since 1906. Although most of the bikes they make are destined for city streets their reputation as a manufacturer was carved out by their flagship world-class tourers. In the UK their legendary Super Galaxy is the benchmark by which all other touring bikes are judged. Dawes extensive range includes the Cambridge pictured on page 11 and the Super Galaxy tourer on page 127.

'Comfort' Seratoga »

'City' Street Elite »

'Trekking' Mojave »

'Touring' Karakum »

Portables »

Whether you're trying to get on a train or just into your cramped flat, a bicycle's famous efficiency can seem small compensation for the trouble they can give, especially when short-sighted architects and train operators get in on the conspiracy. Which is a great shame, as the bike is the undisputed king of the short-distance journey, and so should be ideal for people living in densely-populated areas.

So, how about a bike you can fold up and put in a bag? Forget the old image of the folder as a heavyweight bundle of loose-fitting tubes that you need a degree in mechanical engineering and a spare weekend to fold. Today's folders are different. The best of them ride like conventional uprights and fold to a compact bundle. The use of new materials and frame designs means they are light and responsive. Kitted out with quality components, and often with suspension, you can ride them comfortably all day.

The only problem with them is that you're likely to draw such an admiring crowd when you deftly unfold your pride and joy at a busy station that the time you've saved by having one may well be spent answering the questions of awe-struck onlookers!

There is inevitably an area of compromise, between a bicycle's ability to fold and its ride quality, and so the best folders are, of course, those which do both well. There is huge variety. Some models need a minute or three to fold down, others fold a matter of a few seconds. Some are great for round-town, others you could race on. Some have small wheels combined with suspension, others are just standard bikes which fold in the middle. You have to set your own priorities, which might include comfort, handling, weight, ease and speed of folding, size when folded, and of course, cost. The challenge of meeting these needs has fascinated many an experienced designer. But a folding bike can allow us achieve something which is otherwise near impossible – it allows us to mix and match our modes of transport in a way that is impossible without it. Genuine multi-modal travel. Plane – bike – train – bike – automobile – bike – boat. Bike.

Many folders are bought by practically-minded people who would run away from the notion of 'cycling as lifestyle'. At the other extreme are folder enthusiasts have developed their own sub-culture, clubs and events. Owners' motivations may vary, but there's little can beat the sheer practicality of jumping off a train and onto your unfolded bike, as fellow travellers queue for taxis and buses. There is a pleasant ironic appeal to pedalling it past a traffic jam of cars, worth millions of pounds, all that horsepower going to waste.

Folders have other virtues. Bike security is no longer a major issue – fold it up and take it inside. In urban conditions small wheels give tremendous manoeuvrability, though they may not cope so well with potholes and ill-sited drain covers. Small wheels mean a harder ride, and many folders come with suspension as standard, using the pivoting suspension members as part of the folding sequence.

Folders have come of age. They used to be so few and far between that owners would wave enthusiastically to one another in passing but folders have moved beyond niche, through trendy and into general utility. They are now found on every city's streets. They have made a huge difference to people's lives, and there are still talented engineers coming up with radical, practical, enjoyable designs.

English Cycles
Folding 29er Mountain Bike

For more information on portable bikes visit
www.cyclorama.net/portables

Brompton M3L »

What can be written about the Brompton folding bike which hasn't already been said? Considered by many to be the world's best folding bike — it folds from a small package very quickly and easily (when you know how) and rides exceedingly well — skilfully juggling the compromises which face every folding bicycle. Bromptons are often perceived as costly, especially in comparison to other folding bikes, but their build quality and standard of assembly set them squarely in

the 'bike for life' category. These machines are designed to be used every day and built to last. Although every single component has changed since its launch in the early eighties the design itself has hardly changed, a testament to the 'rightness' of the original concept. With demand always ahead of supply secondhand prices are always buoyant. Great news for owners who've made the investment. Bad news if you were hoping to find a cheap one.

Pacy 20" »

In the world of folding bikes ride quality must be traded against folded size; tall wheels roll faster, small wheels fold smaller. The Pacy 20 is the most compact in a range which includes bikes with 26" and 28" wheels. The rear triangle does two jobs, as a major component of the folding mechanism and as the rear suspension swing-arm. The suspension restores some of the rolling resistance losses inherent in small wheels. This is a quality bike combining a good fold, a comfortable ride, and a very decent performance.

Airnimal Chameleon »

The use of modern materials, built-in suspension and smaller wheels delivers high performance machines which roll, ride and handle just as well as conventional bikes, but which can also be dramatically reduced in size for stowage or storage. The Airnimal is so versatile that, with small modifications to the specification, the same bike that can be used for doing the shopping can complete a world tour and even be ridden to a Bronze Medal in the World Triathlon Championships.

Pacific iF Mode »

Designer Mark Sanders (who also designed the iconic
Strida folder) has created in the IF Mode a bicycle
which looks unlike anything else on the road. It's
aimed squarely at a new generation of riders whose
appreciation of design is informed by everything from
modern electronic goods to automotive styling.
There's no shortage of 'eye candy' in the area of
designer bikes, but very few of them are capable of
being put into production, let alone ridden. The multi-
award winning IF Mode is the brilliant exception.

The limited edition Moulton 60. Inspired by the very first 'F Frames' of the 1960s, only 191 will be made, each with an individually numbered head badge. »
Lower image: Moulton Speed

Moulton Bicycles
AM GT »

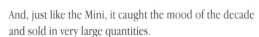

Without Dr. Alex Moulton's revolutionary suspension system, Issigoni's Austin Mini might never have been. Moulton realised that the same principals which made the Mini such a triumph of packaging could be applied to the bicycle and he launched the first of his radical full-suspension small-wheeled bikes in 1962.

And, just like the Mini, it caught the mood of the decade and sold in very large quantities.

In the half century since, Moulton bicycles have been pedalled across mountain ranges and continents, won track races and set international speed records.

The space-frame design lends itself to the incorporation

of a joint in the middle. These 'separable' Moultons are more easily transported on trains and in cars than big wheeled alternatives.

Combining high performance with portability, for those seeking beautiful hand-made British bicycles there is an extensive range of Moulton bicycles to choose from.

Pedals for the People »

New ways to persuade

Jim McGurn tells the story of Get Cycling, a community interest company with what is possibly the most unusual bike collection in the world.

Most people don't discover just how magic cycling can be unless you put them on a saddle and say 'Pedal!' We had this idea for a bike try-out roadshow which would tour the UK with twenty or so representative bikes, with some exotic stuff thrown in to attract the crowds and lighten the atmosphere.

We called ourselves Company of Cyclists, since we began with 150 cyclist-shareholders, and the brand we thought up was 'Get Cycling!' That bit was easy. The next 18 months were to be a whirlwind of putting fleets of bikes together, converting old buses and unrelenting business development.

Eleven years later we're still at it. The public ride the bikes for free, and we give out advice and factsheets. We work mainly for local authorities and schools. On busy summer weekends we can have five different roadshow units operating in different cities of the UK. However, winters are lean, with little income for six months. It gives us a chance to refurbish the bikes and equipment, and we take in local cycle repairs.

We've 'done' city centres, hospital car parks, leisure centres, seaside promenades, special schools, shopping centres, colleges, universities, corporate offices, and even the Inland Revenue. We have seen a very diverse society: from the business people of Guernsey to disaffected young people in Belfast. And we got them all on bikes!

These days the market has changed. We still do try-out shows, but often to specifically publicise one of our workplace cycle loan and support programmes, such as BikeBoost. For example in Sheffield, a very hilly northern industrial city with little remaining cycling culture, we have the task of lending commuter bikes to 800 novice cyclists, giving them full support during four-week loan periods. Some of

our loan bikes in Sheffield are electric-assist, to cope with the hills. Probably our most enjoyable work is in schools, where we operate partly in the classroom and partly with bikes on the school yard. It's sometimes sad to come across children who have never been on a bike before, but great to bring so much cycling fun to young people.

A few years back we began offering something new to our local authority clients: a pedal-powered delivery and distribution service called Green-Link. Once they were set up and working well we sold them to the young people who were running them. We've also diversified into special needs work, under the banner

Bikes not Barriers. We try to keep an example of every special needs bike, and that's a lot of hardware.

All this activity needs a lot of bikes. We generally have around 600 of them, a third of which might be classed as specialised or exotic. We have, for example, ten bikes with more than two seats, two of them with seven seats. It's a great feeling to be surrounded daily by so much amazing kit, until you reflect on the fact that if it's all back at base there must be something wrong: it should be out there earning its living!

At the end of 2008 we set Get Cycling up as a registered community interest company and transferred all of Company of Cyclists' work, assets and staff into

the new organisation. This was all thanks to a loan from a government social enterprise investment agency. This is how Company of Cyclists, after eight hard years of cycling events and programmes, found the freedom and finance to begin a new adventure: the establishment of cyclorama.net, and the publishing of the very book you are reading! Both organisations continue to work closely together. Meanwhile the economic recession has brought big cuts in public sector expenditure, so Get Cycling has reacted by setting up a new bike shop as part of its warehouse in York, and by positioning itself as a national centre of excellence for special needs cycling.

Family and Children's Cycles »

For families who want to cycle together the range of machines for parents to carry their kids has never been so good.

Trailer-bikes, Tandems, Child-trailers, Child-seats, 'Bakfietsen', 'Mamafietsen'. Well-designed cycling products aimed at the needs of young families can be an integral part of a compromise between protection and stimulating the child's sense of independence. You can take children with you on trailer-bikes and tandems to encourage them to develop their cycling skills, while the youngest can enjoy the fun from a childseat or trailer. Such combinations can give children a thrilling sense of speed and ease at an age when they would be struggling to keep up on their own bike.

You need to think carefully about your children's needs, which will change with age. Do you really want a double-trailer, when one of your charges is almost ready to step up to a trailer-bike? You also need to look at what it is you want to do: buzzing round town, day-trips, or maybe combining cycling with driving or public transport.

So what are the options?

Enthroned on a bicycle child-seat children can offer a running commentary on both the surroundings and the performance of the parental power-unit. There are many child-seats on the market, for the front and back of the bike, and they vary enormously in quality and age-suitability.

A practical and more stable alternative is a child-carrying trailer. These carry one or two children, with boot-room for luggage. Or you can fill them entirely with shopping on the way back from the nursery. They attach to your bike only when needed. On a tandem or trailer-bike children

experience the exhilaration of speeding along under combined power. A shared machine also allows an adult to power a weary child home. A trailer-bike is essentially half a bicycle which attaches to rear of the parent's cycle, and can be swapped from bike to bike. You can use your bike as a solo whenever you need. On a trailer-bike your child is active, but remains under your control, watching what you can do and developing traffic sense. If she tires she can freewheel and be towed along. If she has energy to spare, she can contribute a surprising amount of power.

A low-backed tandem with an extra long seat post can accommodate adults on the rear, as well as children. Tandems can also take a childseat and tow trailers. There is a huge variety of configurations: some tandems are also tricycles, some are recumbent, and some for special needs are steered by the rear rider.

The more your children begin to enjoy cycling, the more worthwhile it will become to invest in special machines such as tandems – even for a few years of intensive use by a growing family, for they have a good resale value if they've been well looked after.

Another excellent family vehicle is the child-carrying tricycle. Unlike a bicycle with a child seat, trikes don't present problems of balance. You are safe on slippery roads, can ride easily at very slow speeds and you can park anywhere, leaving your child in place, with the parking brake on. Trikes come in all shapes and sizes. Most have two wheels at the back. This gives room for one or two child-seats behind, plus a carrying space between the rear

Trailer-bikes are designed to be fitted to any conventional bike »

wheels, and a familiar steering arrangement at the front. Child-carrying box trikes transport your children in a box in front of you and you can see what they are up to.

The 'safety' of the motor-car means isolation from the world outside, and passive, dependent travel. So getting children out of cars helps give them a new quality of life. Also, the demand for a safe cycling environment for children will bring improvements for all age groups. Streets with reduced traffic volumes, lower traffic speeds and traffic-free sections will create breathing space for the whole community.

» Choose a seat which has head support - children often fall asleep on rides.

Bikes for Children

Early tricycles teach steering and pedalling, but bicycle riding is all about balance. Making it fun is the key to success. Teaching children to ride bikes is one of life's most memorable experiences. Start on an open, gentle slope so your child can learn to balance and coast before pedalling. Your child should be able to sit on the saddle with both feet flat on the ground and knees slightly bent. The bike can then be used as a hobby-horse or scooter, with the feet always ready to stop a fall. Remove the pedals at first, so that the feet can swing freely. Of course, you can skip this stage if your child enjoyed a trainer bike when very young. Made of wood or metal, trainer bikes have no pedals. They are propelled by pushing feet against the ground, teaching balance from day one. Once they've outgrown it they'll take to riding a full bicycle instantly. Supermarket bikes

are certainly cheap, but they are cheap for a reason and it's because they are rubbish. Buying cheap is a false economy and could even put a child off cycling for life. Cheap bikes are heavy. Some weigh as much an adult's bike. Children are very small 'motors' with significantly less strength and stamina than an adult so don't hobble them with a heavy lump which might be better served as a boat anchor. Everyone deserves a nice lightweight bike, kids especially.

And everyone deserves brakes which work... Above all beware of bikes which must be self-assembled. It takes a qualified cycle mechanic around 45 minutes to assemble a bike properly from a box with all the facilities of a bicycle workshop to hand. What hope does the amateur have of putting it together properly on the kitchen floor?

For best advice go to a proper cycle shop rather than a

toy shop or department store. They offer many more wheel and frame size options, they can often fit a child to a bike that will last and fit safely for several years, which cannot usually be said of 'toy shop' bikes! The longer a bicycle lasts and safely fits, the less it ultimately costs.

Get involved, as much as you can, in your children's cycling. Teach them how to care for their bikes and they'll develop a good understanding how things work. Cycling is a life-long activity and children soon appreciate that their bicycle is not just a toy, but also a means of transportation.

Ride with them often, set a good example, and they'll soon learn how to ride safely. Safety is – naturally – top priority but don't wrap the little treasures in cotton wool. A good well functioning bicycle combined with proper training is better than all of the safety gear in the world.

For more information on family and children's bikes visit **www.cyclorama.net/family**

For more information on family and children's bikes visit **www.cyclorama.net/children**

Steco Child Seat Systems »

We love the exotic stuff as much as the next geek, but deep down we know that it is good utility products which really get bums on seats. Useful accessories such as those manufactured by Steco solve everyday problems to make everyday cycling more accessible. Steco was founded in 1928 and they've been making bicycle accessories ever since. Their clever handlebar assembly relocates the child's seat forward, away from the pedaller's knees. Their Baby Seat Carrier will transport a baby safely on the rear rack. And behind it all is a simple, inexpensive product which is designed to expand the possibilities of cycling and make the practicalities of people's lives easier. The Buggy Carrier is rated to7 kg (15 lb), fits virtually every bicycle and leaves more than enough room for a childseat and pannier bags. How else could you safely transport a buggy on a bike?

FR8 from WorkCycles »

The Fr8 from Amsterdam's famous Workcycles may be configured as a smart street bike, a cargo bike or, as shown here, a family bike for four — and any variant between. This ability to alter the bike's capabilities as a family grows, and its needs change, was a key part of the original design brief. The Fr8's signature feature, the radically sloping seat tube,

neatly reduces the reach as the seat is lowered, increasing it when raised. It also changes the effective seat tube angle. This special geometry, called Adaptive Seat Tube (AST) was developed following a study of seat angles of people of different heights. It allows two adults of even wildly disparate sizes to comfortably ride the same bike.

The matter of reach and handlebar/knee clearance is also of particular importance for a bike that's not only one-size-really-fits-all but also frequently ridden with various types of child seats and saddles behind the handlebar. Made in Holland, the Fr8's immense versatility is finding fans all over the world.

Buddy Bike »

When a child grows too big for a baby seat but is still too small to ride their own bike, riding with the child behind on a regular tandem or trailer-bike can be a stressful experience. The Buddy Bike is a tandem bicycle which places the 'stoker' in the front seat while the 'captain' sits behind controlling the steering. On the Buddy Bike, children feel that they are in charge whilst encircled within the reassuring arms of the parent or carer. The Buddy Bike is a great way for children to learn how to cycle safely, exercise and enjoy real quality family time. It is much shorter than a regular tandem, making it more manoeuvrable, and has a lower front seat so that both riders can safely enjoy the view. Communication is easier, allowing for real conversations rather than half-heard sentences drowned out by traffic noise or lost on the wind. An independent evaluation by the National Lekotek Center, USA reported that: 'Riding the Buddy Bike can be empowering for children and adults with special needs'. The Buddy Bike's layout is particularly suitable for children with autism, Down's, those with vision or hearing impairment and other minor physical disabilities for whom opportunities to experience the therapeutic benefits of physical exercise would otherwise be unavailable.

« A, Ru, Cyril & Sam

=

« Kinderpod from Nijland

With space for four children in the cavernous load bay and an option for two more on an extended rear rack, the 'Kinderpod' is a serious piece of child moving equipment. Ackerman steering, a nifty combined parking brake and anti-tip device and Sturmey Archer five-speed hub with reverse gear complete the spec.

When Nijland set out to produce a new range of cargo and child carrying bicycles and tricycles they were determined to keep the costs down. They teamed up with Workcycles to create a modular frame system which minimises the number of individual components they have to make. Reducing the number of variables reduces the cost to the consumer. The machines all split in the middle, and they're designed so that the sub-assemblies are interchangeable. The machines may be set up as bikes or trikes, as lockable cargo carriers or as child carriers simply by juggling the components.

Taga ≫ =

The brilliant solution to the problem of what to do with your child and child carrying tricycle once you've pedalled to your destination: a child carrying tricycle which transforms, in a matter of seconds, into a jogger. We like to think of it as a trike you can sneak into shops!
Made of aluminium alloy, it's light and easy to pedal. No kids? It's still a great trike for many purposes.

Piccolo Trailercycle by Burley ≫ 🇺🇸

Trailer bikes allow parent and progeny to pedal together, removing the stress associated with herding erratic and wobbly children. They convert a regular bike into a 'kiddy-back' tandem and, just like a regular tandem, they allow humans of very different capabilities to ride at the same speed. Most are single wheel with one seat but there are two-wheeled and twin-seat versions available, and even trailer bikes for adults.

Multi-functional Child Carriers
by Chariot »

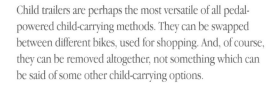

Child trailers are perhaps the most versatile of all pedal-powered child-carrying methods. They can be swapped between different bikes, used for shopping. And, of course, they can be removed altogether, not something which can be said of some other child-carrying options.

Taking this versatility to a whole new level is Canadian company Chariot. Their products are more accurately described as multi-functioning child carriers, of which only one of their modes is a bike trailer. A pair of small front wheels may be bolted in to convert to a stroller, or a larger

single wheel morphs it into a more long-legged jogger. For more adventurous types there's a harness kit for hiking and the addition of a pair of skis in place of the wheels converts it for use in snow.

Adventure Zooom 🇬🇧
Balance
Bike »

Humans evolved to balance. It's why we can run in circles, hop skip and jump without falling over. For very young ones however, learning to ride a bike requires a leap of understanding which is only complicated by the need to pedal at the same time. Balance bikes have no pedals, so they simplify the learning process immensely. By separating the tasks of steering and pedalling they make the step up to pedal bikes very much easier to reach. Most children, even very young ones, can learn to ride one in less than half an hour. The Adventure Zooom is suitable for an age range of around two to four years. It features many of the performance features we've come to expect on quality grown-up's bikes such as lightweight 6061 aluminium frame and rims. These are not mere toys, they are entirely valid in their own right as miniature modes of transport for tiny tots.

Montego » ═
Rasberry

In countries where utility cycling is taken seriously it doesn't come as a surprise that they take kids' bikes seriously too. Bikes with brakes which work, with decent carrying capacity and easy-to-use gears are not the sole preserve of adults. Real bicycles, not toys. If we want kids to enjoy cycling enough to keep pedalling all the way to adulthood these are the kind of bikes they should be riding.

» Family Cycling in Amsterdam
on a four seater Onderwater

Photo: Marc van Woudenberg

Tandems »

Twice the fun!

Some couples love them, some worry about the strain a tandem might have on their relationship. Whatever your perception of tandem bicycles there's no denying their advantages. Two (or more) riders of even wildy unequal strength and stamina can ride at their own pace but stay together. Each rider contributes what they can and no-one gets left behind. The thing you'll really notice if you ever try to keep up with one is that tandems can travel a good deal faster than a solo and this is because they have twice the number of legs with about the same aerodynamic drag. It is for these reasons of togetherness and efficiency that tandems are so often the bike of choice for couples or families embarking on long tours.

There is a huge variety of quality and purpose, as with all bikes. There are tandem versions of almost every form of cycle you can imagine: for road and off-road, for leisure or competition. Tricycles, recumbents, folders, wheelchair tandems, children's tandems, low-back tandems, side-by-side 'sociable' tandems, brakeless fixed-wheel tandems for the velodrome, even tandems which convert into cargo bikes with the turn of a couple of quick-release levers.

Tandems are not just two solo bikes welded together, they are specially designed to cope with all the extra stresses and strains with stronger wheels, brakes and frames. Twice the pedalling load through a transmission, twice the weight on the tyres and double the stopping

There's no spectacle like tandem track racing. Doubles, triples and more were once a common sight at race meetings

power required of brakes has a profound effect on component durability. So they are built to be tough.

The controls are usually all in the captain's hands, though it's not uncommon for a tandem stoker (rear rider) to be charged with the task of operating a drag brake on longer descents. Aside from pedalling, the stoker's primary task is to sit absolutely still. One wobble at the back makes two at the front and a fidgety stoker can easily put a tandem in a ditch. The best stokers are ever receptive to orders from the helm and intention communicated through the linked pedals. Slow! Go! Indicate. Pass a banana... Yet the stoker can also relax, take in the scenery, navigate, back-scratch, activities denied to the ever vigilant captain.

As a general rule the heavier rider should steer. The only exception would be if the lighter rider has much greater upper body strength or if one of the team cannot ride a bike. Steering is harder work than on a solo and much greater concentration and team work is needed to stop and start. It all needs a bit of getting used to. You need to be well practised to have confidence in city traffic, but the open road soon becomes a shared joy.

Almost anyone can take to the back of a tandem for a short or medium ride. Tandems make great taxis for picking friends up from the station. They are great for transporting children to school or into town and they can enable any rider who wouldn't venture on the road alone to savour the thrill of bike riding. Share the delights of tandem cycling with those who cannot ride a solo – those who have problems with their vision, balance or have difficulty coping with traffic decisions. If you want to introduce non-cyclists to pedal-power, then take them for a tandem ride. They'll be hooked.

" Each rider contributes what they can and no-one gets left behind. "

The oVo folding recumbent tandem

Photo: VeloVision Magazine

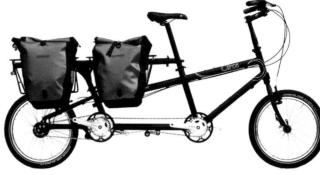

« Circe Helios 🇬🇧

Designed by Richard Loke, the Helios is the ultimate adaptable family bike. Its double length heavy-duty rack allows easy attachment of childseats and/or panniers, but in a matter of moments can be converted into a fully functional tandem suitable for a wide range of humans including very small children. A great deal of thought and care has gone in to this innovative design.

Tandemservis »

Tandems of any kind are rare enough, but triplets are so few and far between that most people will never have seen one in the flesh. Tandemservis are tricycle, tandem and triplet experts. All frames and bikes are original — individually tailored to customers' needs and requirements. They have so much confidence in the quality and strength of their machines that they are rated for off-road racing. And that even includes the folding versions.

Greenspeed
GTT » 🇦🇺

The GTT is the limousine of recumbent trikes. Each one is custom-made, TIG welded from aircraft-grade chromoly steel tubing which is strong yet compliant. It features 406 /20" wheels which are strong and widely available, and tyres are easy to find wherever you are in the world. Storage and transportation of such a large machine would be an enormous challenge if the GTT didn't come equipped as standard with two S&S Bicycle Torque Couplings. For dedicated world tourers up to five couplings and removable seats make the package even more compact.

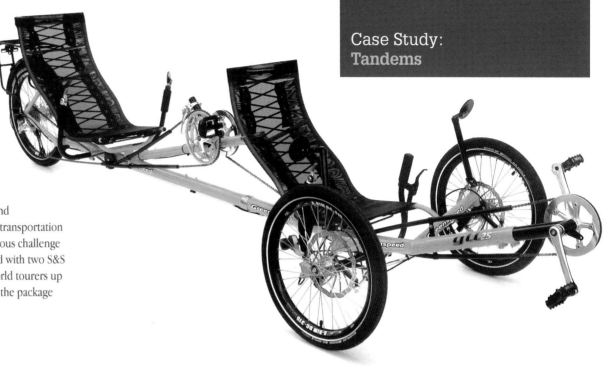

🇩🇪 « Pino Tour by Hase

Viewpoint tandems, which place the stoker in front in a recumbent position, have a number of advantages over regular tandems. A lower centre of gravity gives good handling even when fully loaded, but it is the ability to communicate easily which is the most obvious benefit. The Pino Tour is robust enough for adventurous expeditions with enough carrying capacity for 65 kg (143 lbs) of luggage. The two-part frame can be disassembled, aiding transportation. Hase are the acknowledged leader in this area and their Pino is the machine with which all other viewpoint tandems are compared.

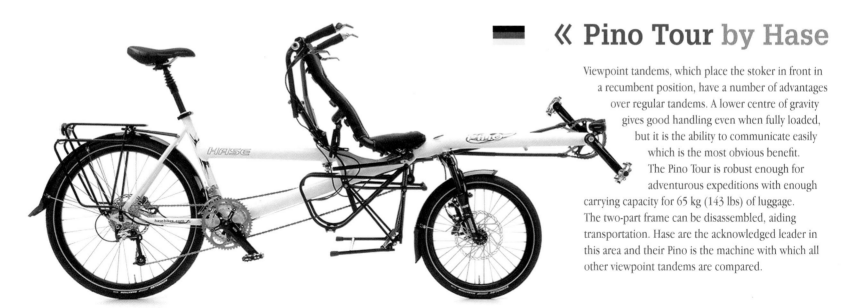

Orbit Tandems »

The Orbit Routier Ultimate tandem is a versatile and capable bike which can be used for everything from day rides to fully laden touring. John and Ruth Hargreaves, owners of JD Tandems in Yorkshire, Northern England, have been in the tandem business for many years. In 2006 they acquired Orbit Tandems and, with their expert knowledge, set about making it the leading tandem headbadge in the UK. Orbit's comprehensive twelve-bike range neatly fills the void between fully custom super-tandems and off-the-shelf. They have

been designed to meet the needs of a wide range of riders, from experienced tandemists wanting to invest in their dream machine to couples looking for their first tandem. Attention to quality is reflected in every detail. Each bike is built around a high quality steel or aluminum frame, available in a wide range of sizes and with the choice of 26 inch or 700c wheels. The Orbit range uses only high grade components and, as each bike is made to order, changes to the standard spec are easily accommodated.

Santana Beyond »

» Five families on a recent Santana tour in Colorado. After conquering Vail Pass (10,668 feet) the previous day, this morning they'll ride 53 miles to reach Glenwood Springs

With experience gained from a decade of racing, touring, wrenching and owning a pro bike shop, Bill McCready became an Associate Editor for Bicycling Magazine. While at Bicycling he produced the magazine's first comparison road test. Overtaken by a passion to create tandems with higher levels of performance, Bill left the magazine to form Santana, a company that relies on testing, innovation and engineering to retain its number 1 position in tandems. In addition to building tandems Santana hosts six events per year to showcase the 'tandem lifestyle', and through which they connect with their customers.

Santana's frames are all handmade in California in alloys of steel, aluminum, titanium and weldable carbon. They make tandems with up to six seats.

At the top of the range, and employing two cutting edge technologies licensed from VyaTek Sports, Santana's revolutionary Beyond welded carbon tandem frame weighs in at an astonishing 5.5 pounds. The Beyond is not only 15–40% lighter than previous tandem frames built from carbon, titanium, or aluminum, it also establishes new standards for stiffness and comfort.

Riding Round the World

Photo: Jonathan Maus

Across the world human power is a moving experience, with the energy of our bodies offering an eloquent answer to the sadness and sameness of industrialised transportation.

Cyclists are everywhere. They may be on world tours, or short trips down the road to see relatives. They may be carrying a hundred watermelons through the streets of Mumbai, or courier-riding in downtown New York. Touring the cycle paths of Denmark or powering over the French Alps in a peloton. And the bike is a great leveller. Whether on a full-suspension titanium tandem or a Flying Pigeon roadster with a design little changed since the 1880s, whether you're a director of a multinational company, a top professional mountain bike rider, or a window-cleaner, it's still just you and your bike out there, doing your own thing beneath the vast and vacant skies.

In Cyclorama we try to bring the worldwide community of cyclists together. In the following section we report on just a few countries where there's a strong cycling story to tell.

North Korea
Kim Jong-il and the Pedal-Powered Lighthouse

The North Korean film, *A Far-Off Islet,* tells the story of a young teacher living on an isolated island, whose school has only two kids. She longs to relocate to Pyongyang to be close to the Great Leader, Kim Jong-il. Island life suddenly becomes eventful, and in a dramatic scene the teacher prevents a shipwreck by pedalling her bicycle so that her dynamo can power up the beacon of the local lighthouse. She decides that her true place is indeed on the island and the Great Leader sends her his regards, praising her as "a heroine of our time."

Had the teacher ever made it to Pyongyang she would have experienced a less heroic aspect of North Korean society: a ban on women cycling in Pyongyang city, in force since 1996. The ban spread to the country as a whole, but has been difficult to enforce.

Bicycles in North Korea have traditionally been exclusively for men. However, in the famine of the mid-1990s it became a matter of life or death for housewives to ride bicycles, in their desperate search for food. The famine caused market stalls to spring up across the country, as starving people bartered valuable possessions for food. Over time these markets have become places where people buy and sell whatever is available. In North Korea today most people, and especially women, depend on this market system to earn a living and bring food home. So if a woman loses a day's wages due to a fine, or has her bicycle confiscated, her entire family will go hungry. Women have become the main breadwinners of many households, as their menfolk are stuck in state factories and other jobs that pay too little.

Where there are almost no taxis or buses, bicycles are usually the only means of transportation, and are therefore precious personal belongings: often the result of a decade of saving. Cycle theft does seem to exist, with stolen bikes pedalled for three or four days on end, to sell them in other provinces of North Korea. There's a bicycle ownership register which does not work too well, since there's no computerised database behind it all. It helps the government monitor private assets. People are obliged to register everything that is not provided by the government and verify how and where they obtained it. If the source cannot be clearly verified, the belongings can be confiscated.

Bikes are now an important feature of North Korean markets: traders use bikes to carry produce from outlying farmlands to sell in the cities. They typically take orders from villagers, collect the goods from city markets, then barter the items back in the villages for vegetables and grains which they then turn around and sell in city markets for a profit.

Up till recently tens of thousands of bikes were imported from Japan, but this has now been stopped, to eliminate competition for bikes now made in a North Korea factory jointly owned by a Chinese company.

Until recently all cycling in Pyongyang was frowned on officially since it made the country's showpiece look untidy and underdeveloped. However bikes are now common in the capital. North Korea has never really been sure what to make of the bicycle. It incorporated the state philosophy of self-sufficiency but allows unmonitored, independent travel and effective private enterprise. It is the obvious vehicle for a country with few resources and little cash for imported oil, but bikes on the streets tell the world that North Korea can't measure 'progress' in terms of car ownership and infrastructure. It could be that the growing numbers of bicycles in this unpredictable state will help form new mindsets, as pedal-power brings people-power under the Great Leader's successor Kim Jong-un.

Rwanda
Team Rwanda Rides High

On the rough roads of Rwanda two extremes of pedal-power meet, as the $4000 dollar racing machines of the national cycling team sweep past heavyweight single-speeds transporting coffee beans.

Team Rwanda is special. They have emerged on the world stage, representing a tiny central African country which is still associated with the genocides which began in 1994.

Out on training runs, in their distinctive team colours, they overtake creaking old lorries and buses, groups of women carrying baskets of fruit on their heads, and men transporting loads of coffee, charcoal, firewood and cassava on tired and almost invisible bikes. Rwanda is known as the land of a thousand hills, yet has always been a country of cyclists.

One of the cyclists they passed on a steep hill was called Leonard, 6ft 6in tall and carrying 400 lbs of potatoes. A couple of minutes after the team passed him, Leonard reappeared at their side, minus his potatoes, and keeping pace. The team coach found Leonard the next day and invited him to a trial. That coach is Jock Boyer, once the first American to ride the Tour de France.

Like the Team, Rwanda is going places as a country. President Kagame, who led the Tutsi rebel forces which eventually drove out the Hutu government, and has transformed it into one of the growth economies in East Africa, as well as one of the most stable countries. Kigali is a city of smart cafes, shiny shopping malls and busy restaurants. Identity cards, once used to distinguish Hutus from Tutsis, now just label everyone Rwandan, and team Rwanda has its sights on the Tour de France, and the ultimate goal of success at the 2012 Olympics.

African conditions do not make things easy. The young men of Team Rwanda live a life of poverty, in houses with no electricity or running water. All lived through the genocide and most directly witnessed violence and lost family members.

The lack of good diet is a particular problem. Team coach Jock Boyer explains how, on average, the riders consume only 1500 calories and about 30 grams of protein per day. To put this in perspective, the figures for the average US athlete are at least 4000 calories and 150 grams of protein per day. In addition, intakes of vitamins and minerals such as iron, zinc, calcium, and the B vitamins (riboflavin, niacin, and B12) are very low. At training camps the team are given a specially formulated diet sourced from local markets, plus daily vitamin and mineral supplements. Once they can regularly access adequate food and water, says Boyer, the team will be even more competitive at the international level.

The team members are scattered across Rwanda, most still living at home with their families. While Boyer knows they train every day, what he doesn't know is how much of their pay goes towards their own diet. This money is by far and away the largest income in each family. It can go towards school fees for younger brothers and sisters, hospital charges for sick relatives, and food for everyone.

Boyer is always looking for new talent. He hooks potential athletes up to a Velotron testing device, which measures watts, cadence and power output. Riders exceeding a given number of watts per kilogram of body weight are given a bike for a month and asked to train with a team member and attend a weekly training camp.

Despite local success, Boyer admits it will be a while before Rwanda — and Africa — can become an international cycling powerhouse. Quality road bikes are still prohibitively expensive. Roads — though vastly improved in Rwanda — are pot-holed and dangerous across much of the continent. And the tactical and mechanical nature of the sport means it takes years for a rider to transform raw talent into top-level success.

Boyer maintains that African cycling is nevertheless developing at a steady pace. Within six or seven years he expects to see the first all-black African team in the Tour de France.

The entire operation is paid for by personal donations mainly from America and South Africa, and by a small amount of government funding. The Rwandan cycling federation has given its full support to the project - the team has even been invited to dinner with President Kagame — but funds are still limited. Air travel to continental races eats up most of the money.

Team Rwanda has been something of a culture shock for the riders, some of whom had never been out of their own towns or villages before. Boyer has also has had to adjust. He admits to knowing little about Africa, let alone Rwanda, before he arrived. He is still getting used to his team's elastic concept of time. Planes have narrowly been missed, riders ambling towards the airport with less than half an hour before take-off. "I got them all watches, thinking that might make a difference," Boyer says. "It made no difference at all."

Tour de Rwanda

The success of the Team has helped the Tour de Rwanda become a fixture on the UCI calendar. The delirious crowds, the festivities en route, and the sense of excitement and novelty: all make the Tour reminiscent of the early days of the Tour de France. The local organisation is considered to be good, but sometimes teams let low budgets show: the Kenyans, for instance, initially tried racing in football kits, before the organiser of the Ariégeoise Cyclosportive stepped in to lend them jerseys.

The first UCI-sanctioned Tour was in 2009: 1,000 kilometres in nine stages, and over 13,000 meters of climbing. The fifteen teams, with six competitors each, included South Africa, Mauritius, Cameroon, Ivory Coast, Kenya, Uganda, Burundi, France and Holland. From 2010 they were joined by Team Type 1 from the USA.

Team Rwanda outshone their rivals on the climbs, with altitude gains of 2,600m in stages of 124 to 163km – but they were frequently caught out in the flatter stage finishes.

Competing in both mountain and road events, Team Rwanda is now a fixture of the Africa pro tour circuit. With a little more experience, they could soon be a force to contend with. The current 15-person team is doing well, recording high finishes in African races, but Boyer doubts they are good enough yet to compete at the highest level. He expects stronger riders to come through: "The talent here is unbelievable," he says. "I know there are champions out there. I just need to find them."

Team Rwanda owes its origins to Tom Ritchey, the inventor, according to many, of the mountain bike way back in the 70s. On his first visit to Rwanda in 2005 Ritchie was overwhelmed by the number of cyclists and the crucial role the bicycle in everyday life. Most of the bikes he saw were basic "coffee bikes", with rear frame extensions for carrying bags of coffee beans from field to factory.

The design was poor and the manufacturing quality even worse. Ritchie founded Project Rwanda, a charity that providing new coffee bikes, designed by Ritchey and made in steel, to thousands of Rwandans. He also established an annual race, the Wooden Bike Classic, for which hundreds of Rwandans would come to race their (virtually obsolete) wooden coffee bikes. Professional cyclists from Europe, the US and across Africa would also compete in a traditional road race on the same day.

The first race took place in September 2006, and Ritchey persuaded Jock Boyer to help him organise it. Thousands of people turned up to line the streets and cheer the cyclists on. The level of interest and amount of Rwandan talent took the two Americans by surprise. Within a month they had decided to set up a national team, and within six weeks they had held trials, selected riders and formed a team read for competition. Team Rwanda has never looked back and coffee bikes are still going strong. Tom Ritchey has now stepped back from Project Rwanda, with operations being transferred to West Hills Coffee Roasters.

The Dutch and their Bikes

We tend to think in stereotypes about Dutch cycling –
but there are differences which can be missed.

Some say that the Netherlands have produced so many professional cycling champions because so many Dutch children build up early fitness by cycling 15 or more kilometres to school every day, in all weathers. It may also explain why Dutch children seem especially healthy, happy, confident and socially adjusted.

The Netherlands have become the role model for any industrialised country hoping to place everyday cycling at the heart of its culture. However, Dutch cycling is also about survival: despite its intensive road network and fine public transport, this densely populated country would congeal into one big urban traffic jam if people stopped cycling.

When it comes to cycling there's fundamental difference between the south and the north. The heavily populated south consists mainly of what is called the Randstad, or 'ring city'. This is a huge conurbation of 7.5 million people formed by Amsterdam, Leiden, The Hague, Rotterdam and Utrecht. The Dutch have built a complex

>> Photo: Henry Cutler of Workcycles

>> Amsterdam football fans on their way to watch the World Cup final.
Orange is the Dutch national colour

transport system throughout the Randstad, of which cyclepaths are an intrinsic part. But the Randstad is a ring of dense urban areas surrounding what the Dutch call the Groen Hart (Green Heart). This Green Heart does have significant towns (such as Gouda), but is kept from major new urbanisation. It is characterised by nature reserves and low-impact leisure facilities. The Dutch go to great lengths to preserve the Green Heart, even going so far as tunnelling a new high-speed rail line under agricultural areas. This breathing space is where the populations of the Randstad go cycling for leisure, and is a superb cycling holiday destination for any cycle tourist wanting a good mix of nature and small historic towns.

To the north are the far less densely populated provinces of Groningen, Drenthe, Friesland. The town of Groningen is famous for having the highest cycling levels of any European city. However, it's Drenthe which is

famed as the 'Cycling Province' of the Netherlands. It's a superb destination for a cycling holiday, with thousands of kilometres of cycle paths through forest, over heathland and along canals.

Drenthe is also famous for the Drentse Fietsvierdaagse. Every July over 12,000 ordinary Dutch cyclists of all ages enjoy four days of riding round the Province, with community support from towns and villages en route. A truly Dutch phenomenon. There are now 60 or so smaller Fietsvierdaagse events in other parts of the Netherlands.

Perhaps the most enthusiastic advocates of Drenthe are the Hembrow family, who moved there from England largely because of the cycling. They now run cycling holidays and study tours for cycle planners from other countries. For more information visit www.cyclorama.net

Germany
The nation which makes it happen

No country has done more to develop new ideas in cycling...

The world is full of creative inventors who think up new ways of using pedal-power. Germany has its fair share, but it's an exceptional country in so many senses. It has applied its best brains to developing new cycling products and concepts through solid entrepreneurship. Graduates of engineering and commerce have taken cycling seriously and built up significant businesses; but they could not have done this without a very willing and open-minded public ready to buy these products. At a mass market level German manufacturers sell to a public prepared to pay good money for quality. At the specialised end of the market this is even more true, with young entrepreneurs doing well, and supported by equally committed cycle dealers. The Association of Independent Cycle Retailers is a network of 275 such retailers, but also encompasses manufacturers, service providers and activists.

Making bikes is only part of the story. There is an enormous cycle holiday sector, with a sophisticated choice of destinations and formats. Scenic cycle routes are signposted everywhere, with hotels, guesthouses and restaurants springing up along the main cycling routes. Germans are one of the most eco-aware countries in the world, and many are now opting for active holidays in Europe, rather than air flights to hotels in far flung places, where they make little contribution to the local economy, and where there is little to do but lie in the sun risking skin cancer.

The Germans themselves vary as much as the regions. The same goes for the local languages, which range from the Frisian 'Platt' of the North Sea shore to the rugged dialect of deepest Bavaria. But everyone understands High German, and English is widely spoken. Culturally, too, Germany is a varied land. Until the 1870s it was no more than a very loose grouping of relatively independent bishoprics, principalities and kingdoms. This has led to the development of all sorts of cultural peculiarities around the regions, which can be well appreciated on a bike tour!

A Special Show

Once a year around 12,000 cyclists flock to the Special Bike Show in Germersheim, a small town in central southern Germany. Over a hundred manufacturers exhibit there, with the emphasis mostly on recumbents, although many other types of bike are on show. It has a great atmosphere, and was founded by a bike store in the town (Haasies Radsschlag). The Show Director, Hardy Siebecke, says that he decided to launch it after reading Encyclopedia, which was a book published up to 2000 by the team responsible for Cyclorama!

» www.spezialradmesse.de

» A bike shop in Berlin, the Fahrradhof, has created a bicycle artwork on its side-wall

Cuba

How Cuba went for bikes - And how it was the only option

Cuba has become a nation of cyclists. Not always voluntarily, but more as a response to the collapse of the USSR cutting off cheap petroleum. It affected everyone – not just because the classic 1950s Buicks and Chevys became harder to fuel, but because public transport was badly hit. 200 buses were taken off the road.

One early government move was to import huge numbers of Chinese-made bicycles, which were then made available on instalment plans. Now Cuba produces its own cycles, many made in the former bus factory. A support system of privately run repair workshops keeps them all rolling. Local workshops also began producing specialised machines for carrying good and people: trishaws are a common alternative to taxis.

The streets of Havana are now quieter and less polluted. Tourists can enjoy its famed colonial and Art Deco architecture by rental bike or pedal-taxi.

The bicyclisation of Cuba has not always been a welcome development. The switch to cycling has been a challenge for some of the elderly, and has meant greater commuting time and effort for workers, especially when they need to first drop off a spouse at work or a child at school. There's also the energy factor. Not all Cubans have enough of a calorie intake, yet need to cycle in torrid conditions to work, which might itself demand manual labour.

In general the bicycle has changed Cuba for the better, helped the battered economy, and given more useful short-distance mobility than the bus system could provide. It has added to the country's charm, and ecological credentials – appreciated by the increasing numbers of visiting cycle tourists from around the world.

Jim McGurn

All photograhs were taken by Robin Thom, for whom Cuba holds a special fascination. He visits the country regularly from his home city of Vancouver, Canada. He has been documenting the rich culture of Cuba during extensive trips across the island for the last eight years. He captures the resilience and determination of the Cuban people and, of course, the ways in which cycling has become a part of the colourful street scene.

Danish Developments
The Kingdom of the Bicycle – Denmark reigns and gains.

B ikes are the bloodstream of city transport in Denmark. They circulate everywhere, busy cells carrying people and goods throughout the urban organism. Without them the city would struggle to survive. Only one percent of Copenhageners say they cycle for the environment. Most cycle because it's the best way to travel.

Cycling is a central part of Danish everyday life because there are bikes which can do almost any job, in any weather – but there is also a growing urban chic attaching to cycling, cycle clothing and cycle design. Young entrepreneurs are pushing at the boundaries.

Planners are coming up with equally good innovations. For example, in Copenhagen traffic lights which were previously co-ordinated for cars are now set for cyclists. This 'green wave' allows them to hit a steady 20 kph along many main traffic arteries. The snow removal policy is also amongst the best in the world, and there are nice little touches, such as rumble strips for cyclists so they can sense the edge of the cycle path under snow yet to be cleared.

At the same time the percentage of journeys by bike has dipped from 18.5% to 16%. Why are one in eight cyclists giving up? A clue may lie in the numbers cycling to school. Bike culture has to start early. Fewer Danish kids cycle to school than in the Netherlands. Government figures quote 45% of all children as cycling often to school, which might mean less than once a week in some cases. In the Netherlands 65% of children cycle to school every day. The Danish may also be developing a cautious culture of safety-first: with strong pro-helmet campaigns. 66% of children under 11 use a helmet, where helmets are a rare sight in the

CYCLORAMA

Netherlands, except on sports cyclists. There may also be a cultural problem in Denmark related to low cycling levels of children of immigrants from countries where cycling has low status. This problem is less apparent in the Netherlands, which has a larger immigrant polulation.

Denmark did not become a cycling nation through its genes. In the 60s and early 70s it came close to giving way like so many other nations had done. The Copenhagen authorities tried to build a motorway across the lakes which separate the old town from the more recent suburbs. There was an outcry, and a general awakening linked to the oil crisis and a budding environmental awareness. Planning switched to bicycles, pedestrians and public transport, with new networks of cycle lanes. The new thinking was reinforced by economists working out that for every Krone spent on cycling infrastructure, the state saves seven Kroner in health care savings.

The Danes are doing well, but admit that cycling is an optional activity. Its success will always be fragile, needing constant support.

Our thanks to David Hembrow and to the Cycling Embassy (cycling-embassy.dk)

The Yakkay, a safety helmet for cyclists which looks more like normal headwear. The makers call it 'brainwear for smart people'. »

Sperm Bike

Possibly the strangest sight in the bike paths of Copenhagen is Captain Sperm on his Sperm Bike. This is actually how the Nordisk Cryobank (Sperm Bank) transports sperm samples to the fertility clinics around Greater Copenhagen. Based on the Bullitt cargo bike, and built by Larry vs Harry, it incorporates a sophisticated cooling system. It is one of many creative but practical uses of transport cycles in the city. Jokes abound about it colliding with another bike called the Menstrual Cycle...

Great Britain
Cycling takes off at last

No-one really knows how it happened, but cycling is suddenly on the agenda in the UK. Positive media coverage, more cyclists on the streets, a new generation of young cyclists buying from hip new bike shops, and a cool wave of cycling chic. Some thank the Labour government, with their investment in hearts and minds. Others see a reaction to the obvious nonsense of mass-car use on a crowded island. Why sit in a metal box for an hour when you can have fun and exercise cycling there in half the time? Who cares why? After decades of neglect and lonely protest, cyclists at last have something to start singing about.

It's not all a frolicking freewheel: immature motorheads are still out there, and cyclists are still being killed – especially by trucks with driver blind spots. But there's a buzz about cycling which we've never experienced before.

"Cycling is seen now... as a frontline propaganda weapon in the war on capitalism, banking, freedom, McDonald's..." So claims motor-journalist-deity (note the initials) Jeremy Clarkson, writing in the same Sunday Times newspaper which elsewhere reports that commuter cyclists now outnumber motorists on many London roads. Cyclists point out that the keenest cyclists of them all are the bankers themselves, who cycle to the City of London by the thousands. Yes, it's all a bit London-centric, but London sets the cultural tone.

>> A fully equipped bike-towed caravan built by Yannick Read to publicise the Environmental Transport Association.

Cyclopark

A new concept in leisure-time cycling has been launched in Gravesend, south east of London. Cyclopark is a 43 hectare regional centre for the full spectrum of performance cycling: but also offers closed circuit cycling for families, for people with disabilities and for anyone wanting to take up cycling for the first time. Financed by British Cycling, it will be the UK's first cycling centre which spans the whole spectrum of cycling interests, though performance riding will dominate. It is hoped that Cyclopark will encourage all cyclists to try other things. www.cyclopark.com.

TFNRttC

Time was when cyclists went to bed. Now they're trundling down moonlit roads in the magic hours between closing time and breakfast. It's cycling's new chic, the LED Light Brigade seizing the opportunities afforded by traffic free roads to rediscover the joys of conversational cycling. It's the nearest cycling comes to being hip, attracting a far more diverse crowd than a run of the mill Sunday club run.

The daddy of all night rides is the Dunwich Dynamo, run annually since 1993 from Hackney to the Suffolk Coast. At 118 miles it's a fair schlep without support – everybody travels at their own pace and looks after themselves. The return, by coach, is cheap, but not quick. The Dynamo's westerly cousin, the Exmouth Exodus, has run annually since 2006 from Bristol to, well, Exmouth. It's slightly shorter, and doesn't get the Dynamo's numbers, but follows the same format – it's for the self-sufficient.

The Friday Night Ride to the Coast is a group ride, run by The Fridays, a CTC affiliate. It's run over 65 editions, more or less monthly from March to November since 2006 – this year there'll be nineteen or twenty outings including midnight starts to Paris and John O'Groats. The FNRttC is a group ride, with regular club members acting as human signposts at junctions and a team of Tail End Charlies offering help with mechanicals and punctures. Although London based, 2012 will see starts from York, Cardiff and Manchester. Registration is a requirement along with third party insurance. Some hardened souls ride back, but most FNRttCers find the attraction of beer for breakfast all too enticing, and, having rehydrated, make their way home by train.

Night riding carries the thrill of transgression and a hint of romance – it's not unknown for FNRttCers to fall in love. Some people do one night ride and decide it's not for them, but others will do fifteen in a year and wait with impatience for the start of the annual programme. You may be a night rider, or you may not, but you won't know until you give it at try.....

Written by Simon Legg, Image: Tim Hall

Canada
The land of free thinkers

《 Street Scene, Toronto

Bike by Sam Whittingham

Sam Whittingham of British Columbia is the fastest self-propelled human in the world. In a fully faired Varna Diablo, he took just 5,434 Seconds to take the world record for over 200 metres, a speed of 81mph (132kph). On top of that he holds the World Hour Record with 90.724 kilometers (56.373 miles). He is also at the forefront of another part of the cycling world as founder, designer and builder for Naked Bicycles, a custom bicycle and accessory fabrication company. He regularly wins awards at the North American Handmade Bicycle Show in Portland, Oregon. One win was for this ornate fixed-gear bicycle blending 1890s-style wooden rims and grips with modern hubs and a front disk brake. A bike which was later purchased by Tour de France legend Lance Armstrong.

The Family Truckster, made by the Bicycle Forest, splits in two to create two back to back recumbent tandems. It has four independent drive trains. Passengers in the rear can either pedal backwards or install their chain in a figure 8 and pedal forwards. The Family Truckster can lean into turns thanks to three pin jointed cross tubes that link the two sides together. www.bikeforest.com

Photo: Brent Curry

Cell phone check, waiting at the lights in Tenjin ≫
Photo: Stephen Crawford

≫ Japanese high school students celebrate graduation by visiting the Hakodate Onuma National Park, where they pedal round the lake on this hired bike train. (takomaruko.blogspot.com)

Earthquakes bring pedal power and innovation.

When the earthquake hit Japan all public and private transport systems were thrown into chaos – so many turned to the only form of transport independent of vulnerable infrastructure. In fact, the bicycle industry did well after the disaster. Sometimes good can come out of misery. Previous Japanese earthquakes motivated the Nippon Basic Company to develop a portable water-purifying bicycle, the CleanCycle, to be used in disaster situations, but also for third world communities who have no access to clean drinking water. It replaces motorised purification equipment, which is expensive to run even when fuel is available.

The company was founded in 2005 by Yuichi Katsuura, previously a water-purifying specialist for over thirty years with Mitsubishi. He now travels across Asia to promote his invention.

The CleanCycle has an intake hose which draws water from river, lake or well. The rider pedals to produce five litres of drinking water per minute. In a ten-hour day it can extract and purify three tons of water: enough for 1500 people. Being a bike it can move from village to village, down tracks inaccessible to motor vehicles

The filtration cartridge last around two years, and the cycle can also be used simply to draw clean water a distance of five vertical metres from wells or streams. The company has produced over 200 CleanCycles and is gearing up for commercial production in Bangladesh.

≫ The CleanCycle was introduced to Burma three years ago and is still producing clean water for hospital patients and residents nearby. It is also used for cleaning medical equipment.

Deep thinking
on bike parking

Cycling is an important part of Japanese life, with around 9.5 million bicycles sold each year. Many are cheap commuter bikes to get owners to the nearest station or bus stop. However, there is also a strong interest in sophisticated bikes, with fashion trends such as fixedwheel cycles. No matter what the quality of the bike, there is always a pressing bike storage problem at major Japanese rail stations.

The Japanese love of the technical fix has led to one of the new wonders of the cycling world: the Kasai Bicycle Park, in Tokyo. Deep below ground is an intricate rotating spoke storage system where bikes slumber in peace and safety. Bikes can be surrendered and retrieved it in less than a minute. The Kasai bike park can swallow a maximum of 6,480 cycles, and parking costs around $15 per month. Six others, of various sizes, are up and running in other parts of Japan. You can see it in action on YouTube (Tokyo bike parking tower).

≫ The Bike at the End of the Puddle
Hikarigaoka Park, Tokyo.
Photo: Ben Torode

United States
Americans go large on bike culture

Sprockettes bring bikes to the dance

Major Taylor Education Program

In 1896, aged just 18, Marshall 'Major' Taylor was already 'the most formidable racer in America', earning up to $15,000 per race. By the age of 21 he had set seven world records and was the first black cycling World Champion. The Major Taylor Education Program was launched in 2008 to promote competitive cycling amongst African American children with the aim of identifying and supporting kids who showed an interest and to inspire them through awareness of Taylor's luminous career, his life and achievements. The program began in Chicago, and reached over 500 African American Chicago Public School students. In Portland, OR, the program reached 150 kids. After one of the most successful athletic careers the world had ever seen, Taylor died in 1932. These words mark his grave:

"World champion bicycle racer who came up the hard way without hatred in his heart, an honest, courageous, and god-fearing, clean-living, gentlemanly athlete. A credit to his race who always gave out his best. Gone but not forgotten."

Only in America? These are the Sprockettes, who describe themselves as an urban, mini-bike dance troupe. They use sassy routines to deliver powerful, entertaining cycling messages at community events on the western seaboard. They've performed from San Francisco to Vancouver, and toured in a veggie-oil-powered bus. It's about presenting positive and healthy female role models, challenging orthodoxies and enjoying the wilder side of life. Members include teachers, artists, gardeners, social workers, musicians, mothers, bankers, nannies, writers, dancers and students. They work as a collective – choreographing, practising and performing. The achievements and energy of the Sprockettes have inspired bike dance teams in many other countries.

The difference a trail makes...

Ring those bells. Even in the US – a country defined in popular imagination by gas guzzlers, highways and road trips – bikes are appearing on the streets again. The number of utility cyclists rose by two-thirds in the last decade, and that covered all income brackets. In some big cities, such as San Francisco, New York or Chicago, levels have at least doubled; in famously bike-friendly Portland, Oregon, levels went up sixfold. Over eight per cent of commuter journeys there were by bike: the highest figure in the US, and one which most European towns would be delighted with.

This research, led by Rutgers University's John Pucher, puts the increase down to better facilities, notably the provision of traffic-free commuter routes. Portland's east side bicycle boulevards, for instance; or New York's Hudson River Greenway, said to be the busiest bike path in the country. (Bike paths have a long history in NYC: they opened the first in the States, back in 1894.)

But the city claiming top spot as America's best biking

city is a surprise to many: Minneapolis – yes, cold, snowy, northern Minneapolis. Sure, its Midtown Greenway, along an old rail line, is a great little east-west commuting corridor – but that hardly explains a thriving cycle scene in a place where the January average is -10C, even given Minnesota's hardy Scandinavian heritage. Thriving it is, though, with all the hallmarks of vibrant cycling cities everywhere: not just commuters aplenty but cool bikeshop-cafes, BMXers, Dutch-cycle shoppers in everyday clothes, bike couriers, cargo cycles, bike polo, bloggers... The lesson of Minneapolis, as many a bemused bicycle journo has come away acknowledging, is that cycling is self-sustaining: seed your city with some decent facilities, and the bike scene will grow.

The economy grows, too. Pucher's team examined the dollar effect of bike trails, and how quickly they generate financial benefits to the local economy in excess of their cost. Over half of bike shops near a trail noticed an increase in business since it opened, with some reporting a rise in sales of over a half.

One Mississippi retailer saw his annual turnover double, from $225,000 to $450,000. A New York shop owner rejoiced that the new trails 'are getting "regular" people onto bikes. Most of these people will never wear brightly colored spandex or buy $1,000 bikes, but they are the masses and are key to the health of our industry.'

The US is a huge, diverse place, and the bike resurgence is still limited to pockets in the more progressive cities and towns. In the southern states, cycling levels are still lagging below one per cent. But with that great American optimism and can-do attitude, things look set only to get better. ~ **Rob Ainsley**

Mobility »

Bikes are for everyone. They extend our capabilities at every turn.

There are few limitations to cycling, because with a little ingenuity pedal-power is incredibly adaptive. Bikes are human-scale and can be fashioned to meet our varied needs. Pedal power focuses the incredible power of the human body, the machine is built around that body, with details of design meeting personal requirements. So if your body's not conventional, cycle technology can adapt. There are as many disabilities as there are disabled people – so the diversity of specialist machines covers a vast range of needs. They are made all over the world by inspired designers and engineers, many of whom are disabled themselves.

The range goes from standard bikes that are adapted to be extra user-friendly, via easy-to-balance trikes and specially designed machines like detachable wheelchair tandems and ultra-light racing recumbent trikes with 84 gears and hand-cranks.

Why do disabled people want to, or need to cycle? For the same reason as the able-bodied, and then some! The able-bodied have many activities which allow them to enjoy movement in the great outdoors: rambling, running, climbing, to name a few. But for the locomotor disabled only the wheeled variety of recreation may be available, and the chance of a good bike ride can open up a whole new world.

The other reason is health. Cycling combines exercise, pleasure, variety and practicality and is recognised as one of the best ways to maintain cardiovascular health. In other words, you can have a great time getting where you need to be, under your own steam, and keep fit in the process. Those with learning difficulties can enjoy mastering a new skill, and enjoy practical benefits. And cycling can make a phenomenal difference to a disabled child's physical and mental development. It offers a magical combination of independence, individual challenge and just plain fun. It also teaches co-ordination and promotes strength, stamina and general health.

Cycling keeps you in touch with the sounds, smells and sensations of the real world. Sometimes the sky moves, the wind blows or the rain falls. Sometimes you stop to talk to people or to enjoy the view. Sometimes your muscles ache and you get fed up. That's what life is all about, whether you have a disability or not. Sitting passively in a car, cut off from nature and community alike, may be an unavoidable part of our lifestyle, but life-enhancing it is not.

Bikes for disabled people need to be extra-well designed and constructed. A problem which would be a minor irritation for most cyclists can become oppressive when even just getting on the machine is difficult.

Lintech low step-through electric trike »

Joseph's Tricycle

When Joseph was little his Mum and Dad had no problem riding specialised two-wheelers with him. But now he's a strapping 23 year old man and his parents' knees aren't what they used to be. On top of that balancing was becoming a problem, and it was sometimes difficult to persuade Joe to pedal. Then they discovered Nijland tandems.

The Nando Too, with its three wheels, gives great stability, and gives Joe a much better view of the world. But it was the optional electrical assist which was the biggest revelation. It has made the Nando Too a perfect vehicle for trips round town, shopping expeditions, and short rides into the country. It certainly means that Dad does not have to give up and walk the up-hills, but the height range on the rear saddle allows Mum, Sally, to ride with Joe, too: for the first time since he was a little boy.

Sally and Joe and Nando Too »

« The Nando Too from Nijland ═

Regular tandems are all very well if you can rely on your stoker to stay safely in the saddle. For carers of people with disabilities a rear steer tandem allows much easier supervision and communication than can be achieved with the passenger behind. This machine, a rear steer tandem tricycle, is just the tip of a model range iceberg. It is also available in a two wheeled version, and one with an extra low front seat for smaller children. There's an electric-assist option – giving eight permutations all together! Nijland's long experience in disability cycling shows in the detail: a steering linkage connects the rear handlebars to the front wheel and the front passenger's handlebars can be isolated from the steering altogether if desired. On most tandems the pedals are locked together: but here the freewheel mechanism can be turned on and off via a handy lever allowing the stoker to be given a break from pedalling. A wide range of accessory attachments such as back supports, harnesses and foot plates enable people with quite severe physical disabilities to ride in safety and comfort.

Mountain Trike » ⚞

Engineer Tim Morgan spent four years turning a good idea into a wonderful new product. He's combined the very best in modern mountain bike technology with an innovative drive and steering system to create a machine which can, quite literally, reach places where no wheel chair has gone before. Large diameter front wheels roll easily over irregularities in the trail and use 24 inch tyres for which a huge range of tread patterns is available to suit any trail conditions. All-wheel suspension enhances the Mountain Trike's bump eating capacity - using lightweight air shocks and sealed pivot bearings for high performance and low maintenance durability. It's a groundbreaking machine which truly extends the boundaries of what is possible.

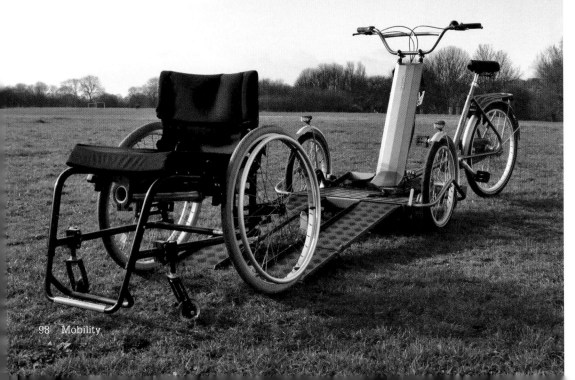

« Nijland Transporter ═

There are many solutions to the question of how to propel a wheelchair user by pedal power. One is to permanently attach a chair as sidecar. Another is to incorporate a chair into the design of the machine so that the passenger sits on an integrated front seat. But if the passenger has trouble getting in and out of their chair these can be difficult machines to live with. There is also the problem of a specialised chair being unsuitable for use by many different wheelchair users. The Nijland Transporter takes a different approach, carrying passenger, chair and all!

Case Study:
Wheelchair Carrier

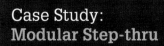

Pfiff Cycles »

Cardiovascular fitness is important to all of us, no matter what our age, and there's no reason why the older generation should give up cycling — it's just a case of having the right equipment. Super low step-thru bicycles are a fast growing sector of the market. They allow cyclists to continue riding well into their senior years, because people can still turn a pedal even when they can't get their leg over a saddle anymore. And they don't have to give up even when issues of balance become a problem.

Tricycles are the next level, being well suited to seniors who need a little extra stability and the option of much lower gears. Trikes also have a greater load-carrying ability, for trips to the shops or farmers' market, so they can be great solutions for those thinking about

giving up their car for reasons of expense or lowered confidence. Pfiff are experts in the area of special-needs provision. Their clever bicycles, tricycles and quadricycles are modular and interchangeable. A universal central frame sub-assembly may be equipped with a choice of ends to configure each machine, and perhaps later re-configure, to suit individual needs. The system of frame separation is so easy to do that it may also be used to make transportation and storage easier. A range of versatile cargo-carrying options and even electric-assist versions are available, too. As if that's not all, Pfiff make great handcycles.

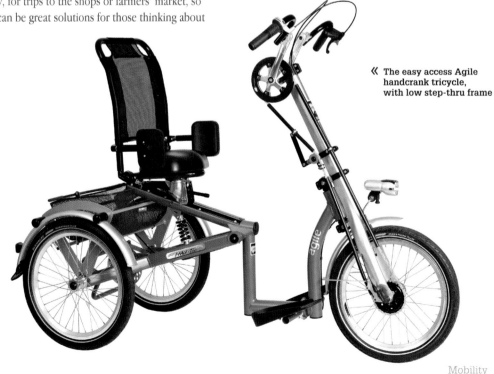

« The easy access Agile
handcrank tricycle,
with low step-thru frame

Fun Bikes »

From micro-bikes to tall-bikes, with a detour around the sofa-cycle...

Photo: Jonathan Maus

Pedal power has always attracted inventive minds. Is it the transparent simplicity of the humble bicycle which has given cycling more than its fair share of off-the-wall inventors? Whatever the reason, there is no shortage of wackiness in the cycling world.

When pedal-power first presented itself to humanity, imagination ran wild. Purportedly practical if odd looking vehicles were designed to perform many civic functions. In Germany a firemen's quadricycle could be rushed to a blaze to deploy its pedal-powered pump, In America a police patrol tricycle was used to transport criminals, secured hand and foot, to the lock-up. There was a pedal-powered fish and chip shop in the UK, and knife-grinding bicycles, once common in Europe, are still found in India. The low running and purchase costs of pedal-powered vehicles have kept classics like the ice cream tricycle competitive against motorised equivalents.

Other specialised cycles have emphasised leisure and fun rather than utility – or the serious intent of their inventors was quickly subverted by entrepreneurs who spotted their entertainment potential. Arthur Hotchkiss, for example, devised a monorail at the end of the 19th century for commuters to ride to an American factory. They powered themselves along a fence rail by means of a treadle mechanism driving a twenty-inch wheel. Such a comical contraption could be transformed into the perfect ride for amusement parks, which is where most monorails are now found.

The dream of bicycles on tracks persists: enthusiastic mechanics around the world are designing their own bikes to ride along abandoned railways tracks; there are over 80,000 miles of abandoned rails in the United States alone. Dozens of patents have been granted for different designs.

Pedal-powered boats have been cruising lakes and rivers since the 1880s, driven by paddle wheels, or propellers. In the 1880s a Mr Terry invented a tricycle

has been held in Northern California in which a number of fantastic, locally concocted machines have taken to streets, beaches, rivers and bay for a three-day 'Kinetic Sculpture' race.

Everyone loves to go beyond the everyday experience of cycling, to create a spectacle, a splash or to turn cycling into a group experience. But there are pedal-powered vehicles which go that little bit further. Tall bikes, micro bikes, micro tandems, multi-seat monsters, eccentric wheeled bikes, choppers, cruisers... Not built for speed or even for utility, they serve no useful purpose at all. They're built just to put a smile on someone's face. There can be no more worthy cause.

As worthy as it is to ride your bicycle to work every day, great as it is to ride up and down trails on your mountain bike every weekend or beat your personal best on the track, wacky bikes let us into a secret: Hey, do you know what? It's OK to ride a bike just for fun!

which he rode to Dover, converted within minutes into a boat, and rowed over the Channel to France, to be arrested as a spy! Since then at least four water-bikes have crossed oceans.

The Americans were particularly inventive, especially during the great cycling boom of the late 1890s. That fascination for experimentation in cycling has returned in the USA, but there is also a great sense of fun. For the last thirty years, for example, an annual event

For more information on fun bikes visit
www.cyclorama.net/fun

Pacific
« **2Rider**

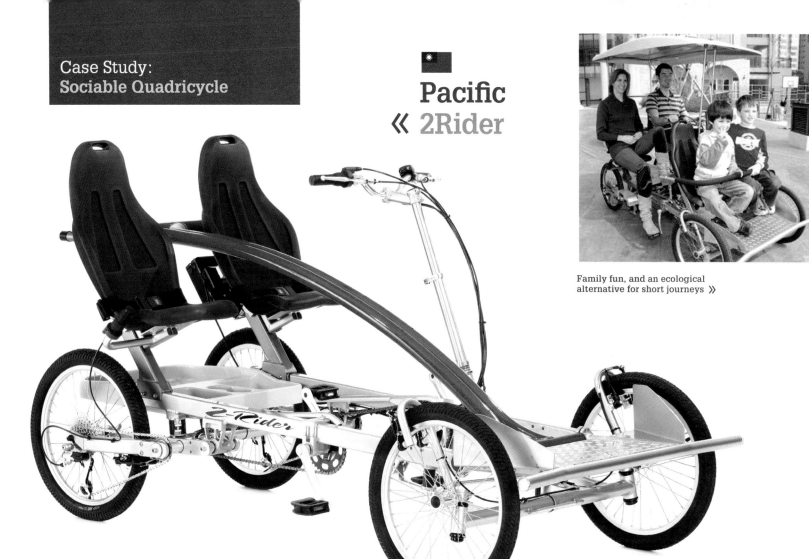

Family fun, and an ecological
alternative for short journeys »

A sociable or side-by-side tandem offers the special experience of truly sharing the ride with others. The 2Rider from Pacific Cycles has all the comfort benefits of a semi-recumbent seating position combined with easy access and the stability of a multi-track vehicle. Ackermann and centre-point steering geometry, plus independent suspension, ensure that the 2Rider handles predictably. Twin, independent drive-trains allow driver and passenger to pedal at their own pace and tough (BMX standard) 20 inch wheels deliver a smooth ride on trails and paths. The use of standard bike components throughout keeps it easy to maintain.

Although the 2Rider was designed for two adults to pedal — with space for optional children's seats up front there's no reason the kids can't join in the fun, too. An accessory rain canopy and electric motor kit are also available.

SN Designs Rattlebone »

In sidehack racing the 'pilot' is responsible for pedalling, steering and stopping. The 'monkey' contributes by scooting the outfit up to speed. On the move the monkey throws his weight around to keep the wheels on the ground and carry speed in the corners. Keen teamwork is essential to gaining a fast lap times. Though intended primarily for BMX bikes, SN Designs can engineer a Rattlebone sidehack to fit almost any two-wheeler.

« Mobo Shift

Perfect for boardwalk or boulevard, the Mobo's frame adjusts easily to accommodate riders of all sizes while the reclining seat back has six angle settings for optimum back support and riding comfort. Mobo's recumbent trikes are a blast to ride and a great way to lure the kids away from video games and outside for some active family fun. They're also easy to maintain, with no chain to worry about.

The Quintette »

Eric Staller Studios
Conference Bike »

The Love Bike »

Eric Staller is an American artist who studied at the University of Michigan and went on to exhibit his work in art galleries and museums. In 1985 he took his art to the streets with a series of mobile public artworks designed to 'break down the gallery walls'. He moved to Amsterdam in 1994, and has shared his magical art with the people of Paris, Berlin, Brussels and London. Staller's artistic output has included some fantastic pedal-powered contraptions, such as the five-seat Quintette and the Love Bike. But his most successful machine is undoubtedly the circular seven-seat Conference Bike of which there are now more than 300 examples in 16 countries.

The Conference Bike has an effect on people that is truly amazing: everyone who rides on it lights up smiling! It lowers inhibitions and after just a few minutes even total strangers are talking to one another.

Ammaco » 🇺🇸
Junior
Penny Farthing

Serious fun! The Ammaco
Junior Penny Farthing fits ages
ten and up. It's a fixed wheel,
just like its grandaddy, but a
700c wheel makes it easier
to mount (and much
less far to fall!).

QU-AX ▬
Muni 24"
Mountain
Unicycle »

The Muni is designed for a new generation of
insane rider for whom trials riding is just too
easy! Available in 20 inch, 24 inch,
and 26 inch — and featuring
extra-heavy-duty components
such as 48 hole rims, ISIS
hollow chromoly cranks
and BMX pedals. With 3"
wide high-volume tyres
these beasts can go places
that no circus clown
would dare to go!

Kustom Kulture »

Bikes and Dice, and Rock 'n' Roll

'Stripped and Teased' by Kram of Ratrodbikes.com »

What is it about humans that we can't leave our machines, our clothes, even our bodies as nature intended? In any field of human endeavour it seems there's always someone who feels the need to push the boundaries.

Hot-rodding emerged in the fifties out of a group of individuals who were motivated by the singular desire to make their cars and motorbikes go faster. Illegal street racing evolved into sanctioned drag racing and spawned the hot-rod and chopper motorcycle movements which are with us today. Hot-rodding was always about making your machine faster and although Hot-rodders have never lost sight of that, over the years the focus has changed. A kind of design language evolved. There emerged a set of (largely unwritten) rules, niche areas and sub-categories: low-riders, street-rods, trad-rods, rat-rods et al. As style rather than performance became the driving force Kustom Kulture

emerged out of the hot-rod movement. Kustom Kulture is constantly evolving and draws its influences from many threads of popular culture past and present. Today it is perfectly in tune with our modern obsession with all things retro. It's primarily influences are rock 'n' roll and the age old spirit of do-it-yourself but always, of course, the internal combustion engine. In particular the legendary V8.

Bicycle hot-rodders draw on all of the same influences as their high-octane brethren. They use the same visual language, the same styling conventions. Chrome, rust, matt black and metal-flake paint. Drilled holes, pin striping and the iconography of the motor racing circuit, the casino, the scrap yard, the tattoo parlour.

The difference of course is that these creations have no engines, only pedals.

Bicycle hot-rodders aim not to go faster nor to reduce weight, improve speed or even, necessarily, make their machines more comfortable. It's all about making your bike unique, about riding something you made or customised yourself. Taking the language of Kustom Kulture and saying something new with it. Cruising the city streets at little more walking speed or just hanging out with your bike-minded buddies. Each machine is an individual (pedal powered) vehicle of self expression – a way of setting oneself apart from our homogenised monolithic culture, but also about being part of a global movement, an exclusive club, a biker gang free to join and open to all who share the obsession. Thanks in no small part to the internet, what started a decade ago as a few guys beating

lumps of metal in the privacy of their own garages has become a fast growing global community of folk who share an appreciation of homebuilt bicycles and Kustom Kulture. Just like the V8 powered hot-rodders the pedal-powered scene has fragmented into many niches: low-riders, choppers, cruisers, muscle bikes, hot-rods, rat-rods and burritos.

In recent years, particularly in the US but with hot-spots all over the world (notably the Netherlands and Germany), the movement has seen amazing growth. And for those who don't have all the skills to make a bike from scratch a handful of small companies now produce limited edition and one-off frames. A few even produce complete bikes. But if there is any lingering doubt that Kustom Kulture has hit the cycling mainstream, witness the spectacle of some of our largest bicycle companies falling over themselves to produce cruisers and choppers.

All apparently unaware of the irony of mass producing bikes which are inspired by the creations of people who butcher mass produced bikes to make them unique!

For more information on kustom bikes visit
www.cyclorama.net/kustom

« Nirve
B-1 Cruiser

The single-speed cantilever framed bicycle has been around so long that it has become an enduring cultural icon. As American as anything you can think of. The Nirve B-1 Cruiser with its 'fastback' frame references the very earliest balloon tired bikes with their twin top tubes and dummy gas tanks. It's one in a long line of cruisers which uses the design language of the vintage cruiser to tell its own story. Historically such bikes have never had much presence in markets outside of the US. Which is a shame — they're comfy, uncomplicated and cool.

Project 346 » =
Basman Luna

Project 346 have morphed the classic cantilever frame into a new shape — without losing sight of what makes the original design so appealing. The result is the Basman Luna, an emotively styled stretch cruiser which offers a comfortable upright riding position with its forward cranks and swept back bars. Inspired by bicycle designs of the past, Project 346 aims to translate classic forms into modern design. The result is a line of products that combines nostalgia and emotion with the quality and competences offered by modern materials and technology.

BMX Bikes »

BMX is still widely perceived as the 'new kid' in the world of cycling but the truth is that it's over 40 years old and an Olympic sport. It's definitely here to stay.

Race »

BMX – Bicycle Moto Cross – has its roots in late 1960s Southern California when kids started riding and racing their bicycles on dirt tracks. Schwinn Sting-Rays, Huffys, Murrays and other similar 'muscle bikes' of the era were the natural bike of choice and these evolved into the racing BMX we know today - just as Schwinn fat-tyred adult bikes were the ancestors of the modern mountain bike. The original frames, wheels and other components were barely up to the job and it wasn't long before small manufacturers started up producing stronger and lighter aftermarket parts such as handlebars, chain-rings, forks and frames. By 1974 the sport had became so popular that a few companies were producing complete bikes. Racing series were organised on the same lines as motorcycle moto-cross (which is where the 'moto' came in). In April 1981, the International BMX Federation was founded, and the first world championships were held in 1982. BMX racing was made an Olympic sport in 2003.

Although racing is still very popular world-wide, the tricks and stunts side of BMX has since come to dominate. Race bikes slowly evolved into machines dedicated to Flatland and Freestyle (with its sub-categories of Park, Street, Vert' and Dirt). Though there is some crossover, each discipline has its own particular set of design requirements. Frame geometry, materials, component choice and other parameters vary accordingly. Although the majority of BMX bikes use the American Imperial 20" tyre standard, good quality machines are now available with wheel sizes ranging from 16" to 29" to fit anyone on the planet. Buying a BMX bike today is a lot more complicated than it was thirty years ago.

BMX is more popular today than it has ever been. Many BMX bikes will never see a race-track, dirt-jump or skate-park but they have evolved into tough, reliable and simple to maintain machines. This has made them the bike of choice for millions of youngsters all over the world — the basic concept of a simple, tough and durable bike has timeless appeal.

Park »

Flatland »

Pure Al »

High end BMX race bikes are rare beasts. Essential requirements are low weight combined with strength. This is a sport which demands extremely high levels of materials and build quality. Pure was established in 2009 to make race frames fit for the highest level of competition. Hydro-formed aluminum tubing optimises the frames' power to weight ratio. Head tube, BB and drop outs are CNC -machined. Their frames are hand-made in Italy and then custom painted in the UK to customer requirements.

Colony »
Endeavour

Freestyle incorporates street, park, vert, dirt and even flatland. Colony began as a small parts company and soon became a fully fledged BMX brand, the first Australian brand to break into the international market. Their first complete bike, the Endeavour, is in its seventh year and is designed to cater to the modern rider with all kinds of riding styles in mind. With Dew Tour and X Games champions on their bikes Colony have quickly earned global credibility and an enviable reputation.

Case Study:
BMX Freestyle

Off-Road »

The mountain bike may be cycling's newest arrival but off-road riding is as old as cycling itself.

The very first cyclists were also the very first off-roaders, until they demanded, and got, surfaced roads. Gliding along these roads these early cyclists had little inkling that one day the same roads would become so congested by other traffic that cyclistsw ould want to escape again to the dirt.

Road riding has been the most visible side of cycling, but there has always been an off-road element to it: cyclocross racing (which is as popular as ever), grass track racing, and cycle speedway all have long histories. The first half of the twentieth century was the heyday of a particularly British and uniquely intrepid breed of cycletourist for whom the lack of a road was little

obstacle. Their bikes were nothing special, certainly nothing like what's called an off-road bike today and 'rough stuff' or 'pass storming' was the off-road journey you made to connect the road sections of a route. Carrying or even dragging the poor bike across mountainsides was all part of the fun. The Rough Stuff Fellowship exists today.

Repack In the 1970s, a group of Californian enthusiasts astride heavy American cruisers began an anarchic series of race meetings in Marin County. Their bikes had just one brake (a barely adequate coaster or 'pedal back' brake) and moderating the dirt-track descent created enough heat to burn off all the grease in their rear hubs. At the end of each run down the mountain they had to be stripped and repacked with bearing grease. The course, and the race, passed into legend as The Repack.

The reason that these bikes performed better than anything that had gone off-road before was the wheel size: the uniquely American 26 x 2.125" Imperial standard. Introduced to the market by a handful of US manufacturers including Schwinn around 1932, and used on millions of bikes over the years, it had a large air volume and correspondingly large footprint which rolled well in the rough and held its grip in the corners. The first few Repacks required a pick-up truck to carry all the bikes back up the hill after every run. The brilliant innovation which transformed these bikes from mere 'clunkers' into 'mountain bikes' was the adoption of new technology which had started appearing on bicycles being imported from Europe. Multiple chain rings and long arm derailleurs provided a super-wide gear range: the rider pedalled back up the mountain. Along came tandem-derived cantilever brakes paired with motorcycle levers. Soon bespoke frames were being built and lighter components added. At the New York cycle show in 1981 the solitary mountain bike on display was swamped by the agents of Far Eastern bicycle manufacturers wielding measuring equipment.

As mountain bikes became more popular, and entered volume production, prices dropped and components started to improve. To many in the industry these new bikes were an abomination, but to the bicycle-buying public they were a revelation. People accustomed to the traditional choice of heavy roadster or five speed 'racer' could suddenly afford a pretty light, super-tough bike with plenty of gears, powerful brakes and the flexibility to move briskly both on and off-road. In some countries mountain bikes, designed for off-road riding, managed to achieve the impossible: making city cycling cooler and more fun than it had ever been before. The phenomenon was set to change the world of cycling profoundly and forever.

Transformation In the thirty years since mountain bikes first appeared in the shops we have seen a complete transformation of the breed. Back then they had steel alloy frames and forks, geometry virtually unchanged from those first Repack Clunkers, cantilever brakes, and friction shifters controlling 15 gears. None of it was dedicated equipment: the brakes came from tandems, other parts were lifted from the touring bike or BMX parts bin. Everything has changed since then. Steel frames have all but disappeared from the middle and upper end of the market, replaced by aluminium, titanium and, increasingly, carbon-fibre composite monocoque. Instead of five sprockets on the back wheel we now find up to ten (at the time of writing!). Cantilever brakes disappeared in the mid nineties, replaced by more powerful linear-pull ('V') brakes, now slowly being sidelined by disc brakes. Modern controls are so well integrated that riders can shift, brake, adjust front and rear suspension and even saddle height on the move whilst keeping both hands firmly on the bars and pointing in the right direction.

Technology Unleashed Suspension has transformed the way we ride, available from 80mm travel on forks for lightweight XC bikes to over 300mm travel on the rear of some big-hit free-ride bikes. Modern mountain bikers now have to consider things like platform-valving, high and low speed compression and rebound damping, pivot location, floating shocks, actuators, lock-out, oil viscosity and axle paths, but the biggest transformation of all is how the breed has fragmented. Once upon a time a mountain bike was a mountain bike. Now we have types to fill every imaginable niche; from indestructible twelve- inch travel free-ride to superlight cross-country race bike. There's fully rigid single-speed, 4X, all-mountain, back country, hard-core hard-tail, dirt-jump or fully loaded expedition mountain bike. Trail bikes, trials bikes, mud bikes, even dedicated snow bikes. Individually unique, but each one a 'mountain bike'.

Kona Cyclocross »
Image courtesy of Joe Sales

Mountain bike materials and technology have found their way into every other kind of bike. Whether you ride a mountain bike or not – if your road Bike, street Bike or folding bike is less than ten years old you're riding technology which was developed to cope with the rigours of dirt riding. All of our bikes are more durable thanks to sealed bearings.

The evolution of the off-road bike is far from over. In an ironic twist the twenty-six inch tyre introduced all those years ago, the very thing which made the invention of the mountain bike possible, may now be under threat of extinction. The recently introduced 'twenty niner' has been a huge success, widely adopted by mountain bikers for its ability to roll over trail imperfections better than its 26inch grandaddy. But it hasn't stopped there. A few manufacturers are now promoting yet another standard, the inbetweeny, best-of-both-worlds 650b (what Americans call the 'twenty-seven-and-a-half-inch').

Off-road riding exists today, and is so popular, comes down to one three letter word. In their quest for FUN he Repack racers could not have imagined that they'd have such an enormous influence on so many people's lives and transform a whole industry.

Without knowing it, they changed the world.

4T Custom » ▬

Going downhill fast is easier with full-suspension, you can focus further down the trail avoiding the big stuff and trusting that the suspension will cope with the little stuff. But when the trail turns uphill rigid bikes gain the performance advantage. They have no energy-sapping springs and linkages and can be built way lighter than any suspension bike. Rigid mountain bikes are a rare breed today but still have their loyal fans. They remind us that mountain biking was once one of life's simple pleasures. 4T's exquisite range of road and off-road bikes are individually custom made from titanium, a material which delivers outstanding performance at almost every level.

« Merida 🇹🇼
Big 9 Carbon Team

World Cup racers travel with two types of bikes. Most XC races are won on short-travel full suspension bikes, but for smoother courses a competition hard-tail still can't be beat. The XC course is where the souls of many mountain bike companies reside. Direct ancestors of the Repack racers, these are the bikes of which they are most proud. If 'racing improves the breed' there's no breed purer than an XC race bike. Super light: check! Carbon monocoque: check! 29er: check! They are the racing whippets of the mountain bike world.

Case Study:
XC Hardtail

« DMR 898 Pro

Competition Dirt Jump bikes are rarely landed as cleanly as the pros do it. They are ghosted away if the jump isn't going according to plan and take a massive beating when they fall to Earth. All day long. So they must be built tough, but to allow quality air time and complex tricks they must also be as light as possible. The DMR 898 Pro takes its name from the temperature of one of the frame's heat treatment processes. It was developed from twelve years of dirt experience and proven in competition to the top step of the podium

before it was released to the public. Steel is the frame material of choice. Relatively skinny tubes are compliant and dent-resistant and a tapered head tube imparts great rigidity where the frame bears the fork. Central to the success of the 898 Pro is its post-weld heat treatment, a process that allows for a massively 40% stronger frame, delivering a weight of just 2.36kg and allowing for the lightest of builds. The 898 comes equipped with DMR's

own components including their Cult chromoly 2 piece crankset and Pivotal all-in-one, lightweight, super-tough saddle and post. The finishing touch is the product which made their name, a pair of legendary DMR V8 pedals.

Specialized S-Works 🇺🇸 Epic Carbon 29 XTR »

Rear suspension took a while to catch on in cross country circles. Riders couldn't quite believe that a bike which was both heavier and more complicated could be faster. Hard-tails must pick their way through the landscape with care, following the smoothest line. You only have to be overtaken once by a full susser ploughing through the rough to be convinced. This outstanding example of a modern short travel XC bike was the first 29er to win a World Cup event, and the bike Mountain Bike Action magazine describes as the "best bike we've ever ridden".

« 146 X 🇬🇧 by Whyte Cycles

Hundreds of suspension designs have come and gone over the last three decades, driven by mountain bike racing and the endless search for every nanosecond of competitive advantage. The location of the swingarm's pivots defines the rear wheel axle path as the rear wheel moves through its range of travel. Minimising the chain's influence and the action of the rear brake on the rear suspension are just two of the parameters with which the designer must wrangle to create a sweet-handling back end. John Whyte was an F1 car suspension designer before he brought his expertise to bear on bicycles.

Case Study:
Long Travel Trial Bike

Zumbi F44 »

Manufacturers rely heavily on feedback from their race teams. It's long been the case that 'racing improves the breed' and DH racers have their own, very specific, set of needs. Their bikes must be able to transfer explosive out-of-the-gate pedal efforts to the back wheel without wasting any energy and they need to be able to absorb big landings and quickly regain their composure ready for the next. The F-44 features Zumbi's own FPS (Floating Pivot System) suspension geometry which is designed to isolate the influence of pedalling and braking forces. Frame flex is the enemy of handling and Zumbi use high grade sealed ball bearings for a rear end which remains smoothly reactive to bump forces whilst tracking straight and true. Zumbi are perhaps the only DH bike manufacturer which offers custom geometry to anyone outside of their race team.

Niche & Super Niche »

Speedway: Courtesy of
Andrew Davidson, British Cycling »

Alice Allart, Circus Artist »

» Martin Künzler

Mainstream used to be just Racers and Roadsters: five speed derailleurs or three-speed hub gears. Then came the shopper bike and then there were three. In those days touring bikes and cross bikes were niche even if they were barely distinguishable from 'racers'. But since the advent of the mountain bike we've witnessed a veritable explosion in the range of cycles available in our local bike shops. Flat bar racers, 26" wheel expedition tourers, road bikes with hub gears, 700c BMX bikes. Cyclorama.net lists seventeen sub-categories of off-road bike alone. Nichetastic!

For many specialist pedal-powered tasks an existing bike does perfectly well, or can be adapted. Almost any old bike will do for the fast growing sport of hard court bike polo; the perfect steed will have fixed wheel, narrow lo-rise bars, and perphaps a sheet of plastic cut to fit and installed in the front wheel to keep mallet heads from tangling with spokes. Specialist but not particularly

unique, such a machine can be knocked together in an afternoon with a pile of parts and a hacksaw. The recent furious growth of hard court cycle polo has demoted these bikes from *Super Niche* to merely *Niche*.

The tricycles which are used to transport heavy film stock around Hollywood studios are simple 'factory' or 'site' trikes with a box on the back. They are uncommon, specialist, but still only niche. They'll be mainstream one day, of course.

But until that glorious day – the bikes you see in your local bike shop window – mountain bikes, road bikes, city bikes, folding bikes, are mainstream. And, if you have to search further afield – for cargo bikes, tandems, recumbents, disability cycles, tricycles – that's 'niche'. Simple. And then there are bikes which, as far as most cyclists are concerned, might as well be on another planet. Super niche, extra-ordinaries. Call them what you will – they are beyond classification.

In the corner of public parks dotted around the UK and a few other lands are tiny cinder tracks. Cycle speedway started in 1946 as a response to fuel shortages which restricted regular – motorised – speedway. In the fifties hundreds or even thousands of spectators turned out to watch races. Today participation is on the rise – with leagues all over the world – but there's a long way to go to match the sport's heyday. The bikes they race are unique, barely changed in half a century and produced by less than a handful of builders. Cycle speedway is a rough-and-tumble contact sport which has lived outside of mainstream cycling for many years. Its participants probably didn't think of themselves as 'cyclists', but it is fantastic cycle sport. New spectators are always amazed at the quality of the racing. If you're ever given the chance to take a bike for a couple of laps you'll wonder at the skill of the riders: how on earth do they go so fast without more carnage?

The optimum geometry for speedway bikes was settled on years ago. The geometry is steep, the wheelbase short. Tyres are skinny and knobbly and handlebars are narrow with almost 90° back-sweep. They are single-speed, with free-wheels and are geared perfectly for fast acceleration off the line. And they have no brakes.

The world of artistic cycling requires extraordinary levels of athletic ability and a skill set which is out of this world.

The first official Artistic Cycling World Championships were held in 1956 for men and in 1970 for women. An unofficial Artistic Cycling World Championships had been held in 1888 by German-American Nicholas Edward Kaufmann but was largely a publicity stunt to promote his trick cycling.

Superficially artistic cycling bikes are similar to cycle speedway bikes – they have a short wheelbase, an upright 'riding position' and no brakes. But that's about all they share. The gearing is extremely low: 1 to 1, and fixed. The bars look just like standard drops but turned upside down and are attached to the bike via a stem with no forward extension. This allows the bars to spin 360° without hindrance. To say that artistic cyclists do tricks is something of an understatement. Their astounding gymnastic skills must be seen to be believed: wheelies, pedalling backwards, riding no hands. They can do all that standing on their heads. Literally.

Cycleball, Radball in German, is a cycle sport similar to football. Two people on each team ride brakeless fixed gear bikes. The ball is controlled using the bike – particularly the front wheel – and the head. The aim, unsurprisingly, is to get the ball in the opponent's net. The first official World Championships were held in 1929 though the sport was invented around 1893 by a German-American, Nicholas Edward Kaufmann (yes him again). Cycleball is popular from Belgium to Japan and there are more than 400 clubs all over the world. The most successful players of all time were the Czechoslovakian Pospíšil brothers, World Champions 20 times between 1965 and 1988.

Though closely related to artistic cycling bikes the super-specialist machines used in cycleball have many unique features and they easily qualify for *über-niche* status. The most distinctive are high (almost easy rider chopper high) bars and a saddle which is so far behind the usual location that it's attached to an extended top tube rather than the seat tube. Radballers spend much of their time on the back wheel and the sport is characterised by hops, wheelies and bar-spins as riders vie for control of the ball.

A dedicated flatland BMX may look like its race bike brother but their different career paths have made them grow apart. We are seeing fixedwheel bikes built to withstand treatment normally reserved for stunt bikes. Bicycle evolution never stands still. The question is: where will the next *super niche* come from?

Your guess is as good as ours!

Gravity Bike...

Technically Dan Levity's Gravity Racer is not a bicycle, although it's made from one. In historical bicycle classification terms, and quite literally; it's a bone-shaker. Propelled by the relentless power of our planet's gravity these miniature monsters hurtle to speeds in excess of 60mph. It's a relatively inexpensive sport to get into: all you need is an old BMX, some welding skills, a full face motorcycle helmet, good leathers - and the side of a mountain. Starting life as a BMX, the frame is stripped and flipped upside down before being reassembled without cranks, chain or sprockets. Bars, foot pegs and vestigial fairings are welded on. Optional lead weights give the planet a little something extra to get its teeth into. Starts are crucially important, as with other descent sports such as luge and toboggan. As speeds increase aerodynamic drag and courage become the major inhibiting factors.

Fast from the Past »

Cycle sport has always been a thrilling theatre of stars, speed and spectators.

» Aimé Constant of France, Record holder behind motors

» T Colman of the Centaur during the S.C.C.V. 12 hour 1934 passing the last check (206 miles).

142. Cyclisme – Léon GEORGET, routier Français C. M.

» At the finish line S J Cozens 1st Louis Gérardin 2nd & E H Chambers 3rd

» "Blob" Harbour of the Bath Road Club

» Francois Faber from around 1908. Note how short the toe clips are

>> Mario Ghella and Henri Sensever in the final of the News of the World Trophy in 1948.

>> Reg Harris – Sprint Champion of the World makes an attempt on the ¼ mile flying start record at Herne Hill

>> Jack Sibbit & Dennis Horn, England, neck and neck against Albert Richter and Toni Merkens, of Germany – the German pair won.

>> Toto Grassin paced by Maurice Jubi in action at Herne Hill

Road Bikes »

Speed and Distance – Bikes for the Open Road

Photo: Simon Keitch

> **We can all now enjoy materials and technology refined by the racing cyclist.**

The shape of the handlebars is the key to understanding. Reach down into those drops or rest your elbows on those aero bars and the single biggest force slowing you down – wind resistance – is reduced. You go faster.

Technology moves fast in the world of cycle racing, which is good news for anyone who just likes the thrill of speed on an exciting lightweight bike. The designers of performance machines never rest. New materials are developed, and frame designs are constantly being tweaked to achieve that perfect blend of lightness, stiffness and aerodynamic efficiency. Somehow, for the professional road racing scene at least, this all has to be done within the strict confines of regulations laid down by the UCI (the international cycle sport governing body).

We can all now enjoy materials and technology refined by the racing cyclist: titanium and carbon fibre frames and components, integrated brake and gear levers, electronically controlled transmission systems of unparalleled precision. Campagnolo, SRAM and Shimano have spent years battling for supremacy in the racing-component market and the regular 'trickle down' of advanced technology means that even their mid-priced group-sets are fine pieces of equipment. Even in time-trialling, high technology has come the way of the entry level racer and amateur: with aero bars, aerodynamic tubing and helmets, and tri-spoke or disk wheels.

Road racing is big business – only companies with deep pockets can afford to run a professional racing team. It is also a mass participation sport, with thousands of road clubs worldwide running time-trails and races. And even if they never race many everyday cyclists also have a cherished fast road bike, kept in the warm and taken out only on dry days for a fast, exhilarating blast along the road, and for a bit of fantasising about taking a maillot jaune – the Tour de France leader's celebrated yellow jersey. Le Tour is the most visible and famous multi-day stage race of them all, and one of the hardest of all sporting events in the world. The great cycling races on the calendar have a colourful and heroic poetry of their own which takes them beyond the mundane and the showy. Finishing a single stage of le Tour demands the kind of physical fitness, stamina and psychological resilience to which most mere mortals can only aspire. Life in the peloton of riders is crowded and hectic with individuals riding as close as possible for aerodynamic benefit, with the constant danger of crashing at high speeds. And after 200 or more gruelling kilometres, they've got to do it all again the next day.

The term 'road bike' covers a wide spectrum of specialist machines – different tools for different jobs – with time trial bikes at one end and expedition touring bikes at the other. Put simply: speed versus comfort.

Time Trial bikes

These sit at the pinnacle of UCI sanctioned competition. They are designed for the 'Race of Truth', against the clock, where a racer doesn't have the option of hiding in the aerodynamic shadow of another rider. These bikes are twitchy and nervous. They require the rider to adopt a position which minimises the aerodynamic drag co-efficient of the body. There is no concession to comfort. In a sport where every microsecond counts designers and engineers strive to remove every gram of drag. TT bikes are the F1 cars of cycle sport, airflow is analysed in wind-tunnels and wheels, frames and other components are constructed using only the most aerodynamically efficient shapes and profiles.

Triathlon bikes

These are very closely related to time trial bikes. Triathletes, too, require a fast machine with good aerodynamics but with a riding position which, whilst minimising aero drag also eases the transition between disciplines. Many triathletes run their bars a few mm higher, the riding position a little more forgiving, but at the front of the race the top athletes will be riding bikes indistinguishable from Pro TT bikes.

" Even if they never race many everyday cyclists also have a cherished fast road bike. "

Photo: Simon Keitch

» 1930s time-trial in the UK

Road Racing bikes

The bikes used in road races are a little more comfortable with slightly more relaxed geometry and drop bars which provide many hand position options. These bikes run in packs: they are high geared for rushing along with the momentum of the group, lightweight to fly up the climbs yet robust enough to cope with 60mph descents and elbows-out sprint finishes. The bikes are the shape they are not because what we have is necessarily the best shape for a road bike but because cycling's sanctioning body – the Union Cycliste Internationale – mandates it. Much of their geometry, shape, even their minimum weight is decided by UCI committee. Although innovation does improve the breed this is 'formula' racing. Manufacturers vie to get their bikes under the shorts of the world's top teams – it's the mark of credibility for a bike brand.

Randonneur and Audax bikes

For some sporting events the hardnosed precision of a pro road racing bike is overkill. Amateur riders will choose a type of bike which a little more forgiving. They want most of the high performance – the low rolling resistance, aerodynamics and low weight – but are prepared to compromise: slightly more relaxed angles, a broader set of gears, clearances for skinny mudguards, perhaps even eyelets for a lightweight luggage rack.

Road Touring bikes

These are the lonely long haulers of the bike world. They share a common ancestor with road racing bikes but, apart from the diameter of their rims, today they share very little. Underneath the mudguards and pannier racks you've find a robust frame with angles set for comfort and stability rather than performance handling. Wheels are built for strength and to accommodate wider tyres. Triple chain-rings provide lots more gears in a wider range including a winch at the lower end. Brakes are more powerful, all the better to stop you with when fully laden in the wet down

an Alpine pass. Touring bikes are built to carry you and all of your camping equipment around the world – or through hell and high water. Reliability is the name of the game.

Expedition Touring Bikes

These have all the features, bells, whistles and load carrying ability of road tourers but with even greater strength and durability. Often based around the 26" 'mountain bike' wheel standard rather than 700c, an Expedition Tourer can handle poor roads and off-road trails which a Road Tourer would baulk at.

Touring bikes are special. Built for purpose, a good road touring bike is probably one of the best all-round bikes you can buy, but they are rarely flashy. More steel than carbon-fibre. If a time trial bike is cycling's equivalent of a Formula 1 car, then a good touring bike is... well, cycling's camper van. Nevertheless owners develop a passionate, protective relationship with their touring bikes which have carried them along thousands of miles of roads, over hills and mountains, at home and around the world. The longer you own it the better your relationship gets.

A cycle tourist is the world's most innocent traveller. You're open to the elements, you've clearly put some effort into your trip, and you are travelling in your host country rather than rushing through it, peering out of a smoked glass window – or worse, jetting over it. Cycle tourists never cease to be amazed at the hospitality they receive, and it's no wonder. The cyclist is the ultimate green traveller – the fuel is completely biodegradable and there's no room for ostentatious consumption.

Cycle touring is about self-sufficiency, carrying all you need on a machine specially built for the task. You've got the independence to go where you want, when you want. And your speed – fast enough to go places, slow enough to see things – is just right for getting the most out of any place you travel through.

Trek » 🇺🇸
Speed Concept 9.9

The air is our most formidable foe. The faster we go the thicker it gets. Time trialists cannot draught and so their bikes must minimise turbulence. The rider is the biggest parachute so position is the main area of focus. Flat back, arms tucked in. But there is only so much you can do to make a human body *aero* and so 'corners' are shaved off the rims, forks, brakes. Tubing morphs into aerofoils. Each tweak reducing, incrementally, the effort required to plough through the air. A gram less pressure is a millimetre of advantage. Because races are won and lost in millimetres. Of course, having the baddest bike is also important....

« Giant TCR ═ 🇹🇼

As the largest quality bicycle manufacturer in the world Giant has an R&D budget that smaller brands would give their right crank for. Giant has long been a leader in carbon fibre frame construction and they were leaders in the deployment of aerodynamic principles in the design of road bikes. Their trademark sloping top tube doesn't look like much but it simultaneously reduces weight, adds stiffness and allows for a longer, aero, seat-post. This was a performance feature widely resisted by the conservative world of road racing, it's now the rule rather than the exception.

Case Study:
Road Bike

« Volagi

Volagi Cycles create high performance bikes for people who spend long hours in the saddle. Their patented Long Bow Flex technology (LBS) brings the seat stays around the seat tube to connect directly to the top tube. The design allows just enough flex to achieve improved compliance for better tracking and control as well as reduced rider fatigue. Volagi is the first company to market a high performance bike with disc brakes. It also has greater clearances for wider tires which reduce rolling resistance and improve traction and comfort, whilst a longer head tube allows a less fatiguing position. All without losing sight of what makes a performance road bike go fast.

CK7 Audax Veloce »
by Tifosi

In late nineteenth century Italy, day-long cycling events became popular. Participants aimed to cover as much distance as possible and prove themselves audax ('audacious'). These evolved into modern *audax*, or *randonneuring* events, in which participants attempt to cycle long distances within a pre-defined time limit. Success is measured by completion. Audax/rando bikes also happen to be ideal for cyclists who want something slightly less frenetic than a road race bike, but who don't want a full-fat touring bike.

Case Study:
Audax Bike

Norwid »
Skagerrak

There seems to be a cross-over bike between each branch of the bicycle family tree. If an audax bike sits comfortably between a road racer and a touring bike, here's a thing which spans the gap between an expedition touring bike and a road tourer. A bike which trades the multi-hold options of drops for the upright control of flat bars. Flat-bar touring bikes are widely available off-the-shelf or entirely bespoke, such as this stunning custom bike by Norwid featuring Rohloff Speedhub, Gates Carbon Drive, internal brake and gear cables in special stainless tubes and S.O.N. hub dynamo with self-contacting drop-outs.

« Grande Route
by Tout Terrain

The Grand Route is a versatile machine which straddles classic randonneur and traditional touring bike. Fitted with skinny rubber it can cover great distances at a sporty tempo, but add a front rack and swap out the tyres for 32mm and it is capable of great loaded adventures. A Tout Terrain signature is the integrated rear rack. Constructed as a part of the frame the stainless steel rack removes the failure points of nuts and bolts, reduces frame weight and improves structural rigidity.

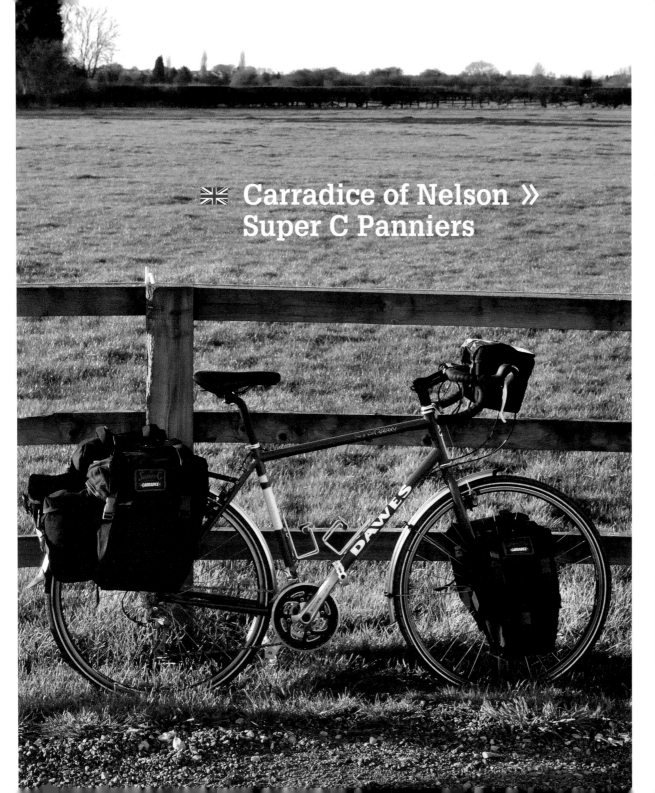

⚓ Carradice of Nelson ≫ Super C Panniers

A touring bike is incomplete without a good set of pannier bags. Carradice have been in the business of making saddlebags and panniers for 80 years. In the early 1930's Wilfred Carradice first made a saddlebag for himself and people were quick to notice that it was far better than anything else available. Friends asked for copies and Wilf's products soon garnered a following. By the end of the decade he was producing tents, rucksacks, sleeping bags and jackets too. From then until the present day Carradice bags and accessories have been the top choice for hard riding tourists and clubmen.

Over the years Carradice have expanded their range to include modern designs, in man-made materials, but it is their extensive range of traditional waxed cotton bags on which their reputation is built. Virtually unchanged in design since Wilf's day, made from 100% waterproof 18 ounce cotton duck, the original performance fabric, with naturally self sealing seams they are easily re-proofed or repaired.

Each bag is checked for quality before leaving the factory in Lancashire, and personally signed by the maker. A large proportion of their bags are exported around the world with a particularly strong following in Europe, Australia, the USA and Japan.

≪ Nelson Long Flap
Saddle bag

Ivan Illich

The awkward prophet ... with a passion for bicycles.

He was an individualist like no other: scientist, philosopher, fluent in at least seven languages, radical Catholic priest (till he left the cloth) and critic of high technology. Ivan Illich challenged the basic principles of western civilisation.

His views were rarely in fashion. He once said "I often have the impression that the more traditionally I speak, the more radically alien I become." A feeling familiar to many an advocate for cycling.

Illich's thinking centred on what he saw as counterproductivity: the paradox of how the institutions and technologies of western culture cause de-skilling, entrapment and dependence. He used the relationship between motoring and cycling as an example of how powerful and global constructs take away freedom and choices, becoming ultimately self-defeating.

Writing long before any serious thought about climate change, Illich calculated that, in the 1970s, Americans spent 1600 hours per year on motor-related activities: including the time spent earning the money to buy and fuel a car, the time spent in the car (including traffic jams), the time spent in the health care industry caused by lack of exercise and car crashes, etc. The average American (at that time) travelled 10,000 km per year (6250 miles). Dividing the one into the other, said Illich, puts the real speed of a car at 6 kilometres (3.7 miles) per hour.

The bicycle, Illich argues, is appropriate technology. It can be owned, used and repaired locally. It does not depend on massive infrastructure such as trunk roads. It can carry huge loads using very little energy. Its use does not harm others or restrict their freedom of choice. These arguments were pure poetry to cycle campaigners of the

70s and 80s, weary of having their mode of transport sneered at. The cyclist could now claim to be at the peak of evolution.

In Tools for Conviviality – a book with a bicycle on the cover – Illich proposed the development of new instruments for the reconquest of practical knowledge by the average citizen. He proposed that we should "give people tools that guarantee their right to work with independent efficiency". He argued that we need convivial tools as opposed to machines. Tools can be used for more than one purpose, in many ways: so a tool accepts expression from its user. With machines, on the other hand, humans become servants, their role being only to run the machine for a unique purpose.

According to Illich, modern transport systems leaves the poor behind. "More energy fed into the transportation system means that more people move faster over a greater range in the course of every day. Everybody's daily radius expands at the expense of being able to drop in on an acquaintance or walk through the park on the way to work. Extremes of privilege are created at the cost of universal enslavement. An elite packs unlimited distance into a lifetime of pampered travel, while the majority spends a bigger slice of their existence on unwanted trips" ('Energy and Equity'). He talked of "fuel burnt in a rain dance of time-consuming acceleration".

He claimed that "the energy used up in the United States for the sole purpose of driving vehicles built to accelerate beyond bicycle speeds would suffice to add auxiliary motors to about twenty times that many vehicles for people all over the world who want to move at bicycle speeds and do not or cannot push the pedals because they are sick or old, or because they want to transport a heavy load or move over a great distance, or because they just want to relax."

Illich claimed that speedy vehicles are a problem in themselves irrespective of the resources they consume or the physical danger that their velocity presents: "Of course cars burn gasoline that could be used to make food. Of course they are dangerous and costly. But the radical monopoly cars establish is destructive in a special way... Even if planes and buses could run as nonpolluting, nondepleting public services, their inhuman velocities would degrade man's innate mobility and force him to spend more time for the sake of travel".

Bicycles and transport were only one of his concerns. He was dismayed at how contemporary society seems to be losing touch with the personal scale of human interactions and the decencies of civilised behaviour. In 'Deschooling Society' he criticised an industrialised education system which fails many and teaches all the wrong things. 'Medical Nemesis' he took on conventional medicine and its so-called ethical agenda.

His iconoclasm and radical teaching in rural Mexico led to a carpeting at the Vatican and resignation from any formal connection with the church. He spent the rest of his life splitting his time between guest professorships in Germany and America, with periods living in a Mexican village working on various writing projects.

When Ivan Illich discovered a cancerous growth on his cheek he decided to self-medicate with herbs and opium. After all, he had spent much of his life challenging conventional western medicine. He lived in some pain, but remained intellectually active till he died at the age of 76.

The machine we really need

From Energy and Equity by Ivan Illich

"Equipped with this tool, man outstrips the efficiency of not only all machines but all other animals as well. Bicycles let people move with greater speed without taking up significant amounts of scarce space, energy, or time. They can spend fewer hours on each mile and still travel more miles in a year. They can get the benefit of technological breakthroughs without putting undue claims on the schedules, energy, or space of others. They become masters of their own movements without blocking those of their fellows. Their new tool creates only those demands which it can also satisfy. Every increase in motorized speed creates new demands on space and time. The use of the bicycle is self-limiting. It allows people to create a new relationship between their life-space and their life-time, between their territory and the pulse of their being, without destroying their inherited balance. The advantages of modern self-powered traffic are obvious, and ignored. That better traffic runs faster is asserted, but never proved. Before they ask people to pay for it, those who propose acceleration should try to display the evidence for their claim."

What distinguishes the traffic in rich countries from the traffic in poor countries is not more mileage per hour of life-time for the majority, but more hours of compulsory consumption of high doses of energy, packaged and unequally distributed by the transportation industry.

Man on a bicycle can go three or four times faster than the pedestrian, but uses five times less energy in the process. He carries one gram of his weight over a kilometer of flat road at an expense of only 0.15 calories. The bicycle is the perfect transducer to match man's metabolic energy to the impedance of locomotion. Equipped with this tool, man outstrips the efficiency of not only all machines but all other animals as well.

In the bicycle system, engineered roads are necessary only at certain points of dense traffic, and people who live far from the surfaced path are not thereby automatically isolated as they would be if they depended on cars or trains. The bicycle has extended man's radius without shunting him onto roads he cannot walk. Where he cannot ride his bike, he can usually push it.

The bicycle also uses little space. Eighteen bikes can be parked in the place of one car, thirty of them can move along in the space devoured by a single automobile. It takes three lanes of a given size to move 40,000 people across a bridge in one hour by using automated trains, four to move them on buses, twelve to move them in their cars, and only two lanes for them to pedal across on bicycles. Of all these vehicles, only the bicycle really allows people to go from door to door without walking. The cyclist can reach new destinations of his choice without his tool creating new locations from which he is barred."

Energy and Equity: Toward a History of Needs. Ivan Illich, New York: Pantheon, 1978.

Cargo Bikes »

A week's shopping? A sack of potatoes? A sofa?? Don't underestimate the humble pedal cycle's ability to haul.

» Metrofiets Cargo Bikes are made by hand in the USA from aircraft grade steel

It's still a bit controversial to carry a big load on a bike in most of the 'developed' world. Why this should be is a bit of a mystery for the inhabitants of some more enlightened cities, such as Amsterdam and Copenhagen, where load-carrying bicycles are a daily fact of life. And of course the bicycle carries billions of tons in many less affluent countries.

Carrying a load by bike is a very sensible alternative in today's cities: it's versatile, quiet, pollution-free, relatively slow-moving, pedestrian-friendly and totally practical. For the employer, pedal-powered deliveries also mean healthier, happier, more productive staff and intrigued,

admiring customers. Once again, human power wins out, when used in the right way, in the right place.

Load-carrying bikes have benefited from some exciting new developments in bike technology, producing strength without crippling weight, a wide choice of gears and brakes capable of arresting the largest load. A huge range of options are available now, ranging from trailers with a 30kg payload to quadricycles which will take a quarter of a tonne.

There's no pretending that 250kg load will pedal the vehicle up a hill for you, but these 'bicycle HGVs' can easily outclass their diesel equivalents in certain

scenarios, when all the implications of motorised deliveries are taken into account: fuel costs, insurance, maintenance, capital, parking and access restrictions.

Mixing with motorised traffic is rarely a problem: the road presence of these machines means that drivers keep their distance and show respect. Bikes, trikes and quadricycles are now available for almost any load-carrying situation: and possibilities are also opened up by trailers and tandems.

Trailers let you do things with bikes which other options simply can't match. Try carrying a cello on a bike, or the contents of an apartment, or a sack of flour. Panniers front and back are great for many tasks, but when the volume and weight of your cargo rise above a certain limit, trailers are the thing.

They can be attached to your favourite bicycle and shared with the family or friends. Some are designed to be pushed as trolleys so you can wheel them into

» Workcycles Fr8

buildings or through pedestrian areas. Some are substantial enough to carry children or to be used for business deliveries.

Even if your carrying need isn't covered directly, very often the stable load platforms that these machines provide are perfect for custom modifications. There is a limit to what can be carried: manufacturers will specify a maximum load, and this should be respected. Another limit is the power in your legs: a lot of modern machines have very low gears, but do be realistic about hills when fully-loaded. Check the brakes before you set off, and take a few moments somewhere safe to get used to the feel of the loaded vehicle. Riding with big loads is a great experience and superb fun.

It's worth remembering that many cycling solutions are dual-use. A child-trailer or box-trike gets your little ones to nursery, but also make great shopping vehicles at other times.

Of course, you can also carry loads without investing in serious technology. Even a pair of good panniers can allow you to carry enough shopping, or luggage to avoid creating another car journey!

» Renso Cruz moving the contents of a bike shop

For more information on cargo bikes visit
www.cyclorama.net/cargo

The Prana by Velonom » ▬

Crates, cartons, sacks, drums, barrels, surfboards, kids... The Prana cargo bike from Velonom is the perfect answer to many personal, family and commercial transport needs and is finding many new friends, especially in towns and cities. The Prana's integrated steel cargo chassis is in a different league from the bolt-on aluminum racks commonly available in bike shops. It can carry ten times the weight, multiple passengers, and has the space to load up awkward objects like ladders, plywood, other bicycles, etc.

It is not a new idea but in recent years this style of 'long-tail' cargo bike has evolved with new technology and a new generation of components: An oversized (14mm) rear axle and 48 stainless steel spokes create an immensely strong rear wheel which allows the Prana to easily manage loads up to 300 kg.

Customers can design their Prana to suit their precise needs. There are three base models and the long list of additional options includes mudguards, lights, puncture resistant tyres and even an electric drive kit which converts the bike into an efficient 'pedelec', perfect for those extra heavy loads or hilly terrain. Cargo carrying options include specially designed wicker baskets, a frame mounted front luggage rack and rear seats for two small children.

Other bikes transport you, but the Prana can comfortably haul your friends and kids, equipment, food, gear, deliveries, and much more.

8freight »

There are only two options when it comes to the layout of a cargo bike: rider in front or cargo in front. For designer Mike Burrows the choice was clear. Traditional machines which carry their load up front require two head tubes, two steerers, two head-sets and a connecting rod, adding complexity and cost. Placing the rider's weight over the front wheel also prevents front wheel wash-outs. Loss of grip on the rear wheel is less likely to have you off. Black Country Atelier, a UK Midlands-based design studio, wanted to bring a new model 8Freight to a wider audience and worked with Burrows Engineering to scale up production, also adding a range of freight options such as baskets and lockable boxes. The new machine uses more conventional parts in place of some of the original's specially machined components, making the bike easier to make and to own, but it has lost none of its usefulness and character. Few bikes are so single minded. This is a serious tool designed for everyday, fast, high-mileage use. As a result the 8Freight has earned a loyal fan base not just with professional courier companies but with anyone able to think of a practical use for it — from mums to window cleaners.

Maderna
Truck » =

Cargo bikes are stable and robust, but they are rarely fast. Mountain bikes are swift and surefooted. Maderna have neatly combined the two to create a nimble machine with a capacity of up to 150 Kg (330 lbs). Mountain bike front end geometry and riding position combined with the low centre of gravity make the bike very manouverable and easy to ride even when heavily loaded. They've made a bike which is strong and stable but which goes and stops well too. Maderna have been producing innovative bike designs for decades. The Truck follows in that great tradition.

« Bike-Hod
Trailer 🇬🇧

Trailers multiply the carrying capacity of any regular bike. They come in all shapes and sizes and are used for shopping, touring and even by people earning their living. They attach in a variety of ways so there's a trailer available to fit any kind of bike.

Bike-Hod have been producing trailers for thirty years. Their top of the range Traveller has spoked wheels, aluminium rims and high quality tyres for a smooth and efficient ride. The Traveller also features a wide track for stability and comes with a high-volume waterproof bag. You can also order extra towing brackets, so you can swap your Bike-Hod from bike to bike.

Folding Cargo Bike
« by Bernds ▬

Cargo-in-front bikes rely on a linkage to transmit steering input to the front wheel. The rider sits behind the load, a helpful feature if you want to keep an eye on (or talk to) your cargo. This is probably the only quick-fold cargo bike in the world. Bernds is a family business which has been making bikes by hand in Germany for twenty years. Their extraordinary bicycles reveal an almost obsessive attention to engineering detail. Their range includes a low-step tandem which can, in moments, fold to fit in the boot of a Golf, and a range of compact solo bikes suitable for all round use. To achieve their goals Bernds have exploited recent developments in tyre technology. Modern tyres are available with high quality construction for easy rolling combined with high air volumes for stability and comfort. Small wheels are lighter and stronger. And, of course, more compact for folding. Lots of bicycle makers are unique but Bernds takes 'unique' to a whole new level.

Pedelecs »

More power to your pedals!

" Electric-assist: like having a gentle wind always behind you "

» Flier/Movelo VIII

The general public can see the potential benefits of electric bikes even if many 'proper' cyclists look away. Globally, electric bike sales have sky-rocketed in recent years and the trend shows no signs of abating. The technology has finally caught up with the promise: electric bikes are here to stay.

The idea of attaching a motor of some kind to a pedal powered machine is not a new one. Pedal cycles had not long been invented before some creative speed-demon wanted to go faster, and the earliest motorbikes really were no more than regular bicycles with engines bolted into the frame. Many well known manufacturers, including Schwinn, Triumph, Rudge, Raleigh and BSA were known for their production of motorcycles as well as pedal cycles.

Steam engines and electric motors were experimented with in the early days, but the world of motorbikes and motor cars has come to be dominated by the fossil-fueled internal combustion engine. Unlike mopeds (small-capacity motorbikes with pedal-power assist) and electric motorbikes, whose motors are their main means of propulsion, pedelecs are fitted with a small motor to augment the rider's energy. The idea is not to make a very much faster or more powerful vehicle, but simply to flatten the hills and shorten the miles. Essentially a conventional bicycle, but one that lends a hand when required.

Over the years the internal combustion engine has been refined and tuned to a very high level of development at vast expense whilst the electric motor has been largely ignored, stuck in an evolutionary dead-

end of low-performance golf-carts and milk trolleys. Now that the end of the oil age is in sight people are starting to look again at the alternatives. The idea of an electric bike has been around for a very long time but until very recently the technology simply wasn't mature enough. Early electric bikes were prone to cutting out when they encountered too high a load. In the real world this meant that they stopped working on even moderate hills (the very place you wanted electric assist!) leaving the poor rider to drag the now useless weight of battery and motor to the top under their own steam. It has taken some really big technological leaps for electrically assisted bikes to start to realise their full potential. Heavy lead-acid batteries have been replaced by lighter NiCad (nickel-cadmium) batteries and then, thanks to ongoing developments in mobile (cell) phone

technology, NiMH (nickel metal hydride) and now lithium-ion giving better power-to-weight ratios and improved reliability.

Driven by the rapidly expanding Japanese and Chinese electric-bike markets, economies of scale have driven prices down and the evolution of on-board electronic control systems and drive motors has greatly improved efficiency and useability. Although there may be some way to go before electric bikes gain acceptance by those in the cycling community who still consider electric cyclists to be cheating, they put smiles on the faces of all who try them. Some say they make you feel as if you have a permanent tailwind, some like you are forever whooshing downhill.

But it's not all a bed of roses. Their environmentally benign credentials are often over-stated. Batteries

remain problematic. There are pitfalls at every stage of their existence – pollution arising from mining the raw materials, their manufacture, and eventual disposal. What's more, each time you charge an electric bike approximately a kilogramme (2lbs) of coal is burnt at a power station, producing about 3 kg (7lbs) of CO_2. Do it every night, as some people do, and that's really rather a lot. Then there's the problem of loss of capacity and efficiency over their often too short life span. Better than a car of course, but not as 'green' as a regular bike.

Perhaps the best way of looking at pedelecs is not as a 'cheating' bicycle but as a cheaper, less polluting alternative to the car. Electric bikes with their promise of inexpensive, fast and efficient personal transport, might just be the elusive carrot which entices folk out of their motorised metal boxes.

Pacific iF Reach DC »

It's perhaps the most difficult challenge of all for a bicycle designer: to produce a bike which works well as a bicycle yet folds to a reasonably compact and easy to manage package. Many bikes achieve one or the other but very few do both well. It's a very brave manufacturer indeed who also adds electric assist and full suspension to the specification.

In the past the choice was stark – electric or folding. There has, for a long time, been a gaping hole in the market for a bike which is both. If a good folding bike is capable of opening up new possibilities in multi-modal travel, imagine the potential for a folding pedelec with its increased speed and range. Expect to see many more of these on the roads in years to come.

« Spencer Ivy
The Ivy 🇬🇧

Electrically assisted bicycles sometimes have all the visual appeal of a collaboration between Heath Robinson and Dr Frankenstein. Spencer Ivy are keen to demonstrate that electric bikes can look 'normal', attractive and desirable. Perhaps even cool. Their classic step-through electric bicycle blends comfort and style with electric assistance to give an extra push when needed. The highly advanced Panasonic motor system has three levels of assistance and is combined with a battery which can deliver up to 50 miles of power between recharges.

E-Hybride 9000
by Ghost »

As electric technology came of age for street bikes, it took no great leap of imagination to apply it to off-road bikes. Using technology from the most experienced electric-drive manufacturers in the bicycle industry Ghost have developed a bike which doesn't shout about its abilities but delivers superior hill-climbing ability and vastly increased range. The electric motor is concealed in the rear hub, the battery integrated into the down tube. An easily legible display on the bars shows all important information. Hills become less intimidating, distance becomes a minor matter. Electric mountain bikes make perfect sense, making mole-hills out of mountains.

Recumbents and Velomobiles »

Zipping along with the wind in your hair on an exclusive machine you're part of cycling's cutting edge.

When pedalling a regular bicycle by far the single biggest thing slowing you down is wind resistance. It's why road bikes have drop bars and TT bikes have aerodynamically profiled tubes. It's why riders draught each other and wear smooth skin-suits. At 20mph on a regular bike around 80% of the rider's energy is being used just to overcome wind resistance so anything which can be done to reduce the Cd (drag co-efficient) of bike and rider will make it go faster.

The very first recumbent bicycles were built purely for speed. In 1934, riding a Velocar with a very laid back – almost flat on his back – riding position Frenchman Francis Foure shattered seven world records. Cycling's governing body, the Union Cycliste International (UCI) promptly banned recumbents from sanctioned racing. The ban remains to this day.

In the 1970s the International Human Powered Vehicle Association (IHVPA) was established to encourage the development of all human-powered machines on land, sea and air without artificial design restrictions. Recumbents are designed for all purposes, but those designed to be fast are wildly more aerodynamically efficient, and therefore very much faster, than a regular bicycle – even a top end Time Trial bike. Today top flight competition HPVs are capable of speeds in excess of 80mph but for most modern cyclists the primary advantage of recumbents is comfort. Longer rides become a pleasure not a pain. Compared to an upright bike body weight is spread over a (ahem) larger area and there is barely any load on the arms. You

get speed with comfort, without needing to crouch into uncomfortable contortions to minimise air resistance. Many people whose aches and pains have forced them to give up cycling may find that recumbents can put them on the road again.

The riding style is quite different. Although your mind will get the hang of it quite quickly your body will need time to adapt: recumbents use a slightly different muscle group which can make hill-climbing frustratingly slow to start with – even for an experienced cyclist. In general semi-recumbents with a more upright seating position are better for touring and in traffic whilst recumbents with a more laid-back riding position are for higher performance or competition. On the road recumbents might look to be too close to car-bumper level, but in fact, instead of looking straight through you, cyclist-blind drivers are more likely to give you a double-take. If they can see the white lines on the road they can certainly see a recumbent. In practice recumbent riders are given lots of space by other road users. Recumbents come in as many varieties as regular bikes: bikes, trikes, quads (solo or tandem), cargo-carriers, racers, tourers, even folders.

Bicycles: Alongside the usual variations of wheel size, components, suspension, and frame materials comes the question of wheelbase. Short wheelbase recumbent bikes are often speedier and more manoeuvrable; the long wheelbase varieties are traditionally more popular for touring, and are easier for beginners to ride.

Tricycles and quads: Adding one or more wheels adds

a whole new dimension. Tricycles can be split into two types: *tadpole* (two wheels at the front and one behind) or *delta* (two rear wheels and one front). The sure-footed manoeuvrability is appealing to many, especially in wet or icy conditions. Three or four wheeled stability is also unbeatable for load-carrying. Windscreens and tail-boxes which often form useful, lockable luggage containers smooth the airflow and can offer some weather protection. But the ultimate accessory for your recumbent is a full fairing Cx or Cd (co-efficient of drag) is a function of frontal area (the frontal profile) and shape. The recumbent position has a distinct advantage over the upright position of a regular bike by virtue of its reduced frontal area but there's little that can be done to alter the shape of a human being. Adding an aerodynamically efficient body shell, however, raises performance to a Whole New Level.

Velomobiles

For simplicity, effectiveness and inexpensiveness there is still nothing to beat just jumping on an ordinary bike and pedalling away. Velomobiles won't replace bicycles any time soon but they could potentially replace a few cars! These fully faired eco-machines are a fascinating concept. They will typically have more than two wheels for stability. A full-body fairing gives protection against the elements and to improve aerodynamic efficiency. They are a fast and efficient, yet human-scale.

Building velomobiles is not easy. The designer has to juggle mechanical efficiency, ergonomics, aerodynamics, durability, practicality and economics. The body-shell needs to be light yet strong to cope with daily bumps and a lifetime of vibration. Visibility, too, is important, as are ventilation and access.

There is a vibrant subculture of velomobile owners, many of whom cover tens of thousands of kilometres a year. No need to carry rain gear to work every day, in case

the weather changes – you have your own personal space, warm and dry. There are even some individuals who roam the world by velomobile: their vehicle is their home!

The velomobile occupies a very special niche in the transport market. It offers an incredibly efficient, relaxed, and eco-friendly way of getting around. And as technology improves electric hybrids are becoming more viable. As oil becomes more expensive to extract it is inevitable that the velomobile will become an increasingly popular personal transport option.

On a Mango to Work

David Hembrow rides a velomobile on a 60 km round trip to his work at Sinner Bikes in Groningen. His choice of transport is fast, fun, comfortable and not that unusual on long-distance Dutch bike paths. We asked him to explain the appeal:

" Velomobiles vary enormously in their practicality. My Mango has 70 litres of luggage space behind the seat – enough that I've gone on holiday with a tent, sleeping bag, camping mat and a few days' food. All of it is protected from both the elements and from the transmission, and it's all within the aerodynamic form so you can still ride fast. It's always T-shirt climate inside the Mango even when it's freezing outside. Except on days when I've got stuck in snow I've never averaged less than 25kph. Even when I rode the 240 km long Elfstedentocht in my velomobile I averaged 30 km/h, and in a race with no traffic or other people to work around I've ridden it at nearly 40 km/h for six hours continuously. It's quite a phenomenal feeling. So it goes like a bat out of hell as well as being supremely practical.

However even the lightest velomobiles are heavier than regular bikes. At hill climbing speeds aerodynamics play no part so that extra weight becomes a burden. But once you're over the top and have gravity on your side... "

For more information on recumbents visit **www.cyclorama.net/recumbents**

Case Study:
Entry Level Recumbent Trike

KMX Karts » 🇬🇧

The super-low centre of gravity and light weight of a recumbent tricycle allows it to out-corner almost anything else on the road, delivering a thrill unequalled by any other form of transport, pedal-powered or otherwise. Historically the low production runs, high engineering values and research & development costs of such machines have rendered them well out of reach of most cyclists' budgets. Until, that is, KMX came along. In 2000 Barry Smith, a former helicopter engineer, decided to build something 'a bit different' for his son Dean, largely from parts liberated from a dumpster. It generated so much interest that they decided to turn it into a business. Adult versions soon followed and from those humble beginnings their greatly expanded range now sells on four continents. Their machines deliver all of the fun and excitement but at a fraction of the cost of most other recumbent tricycles. Of course they still make versions for children too – why should grown-ups have all the fun?

Tripod by LTE » ≡

Recumbent trikes are classified not only by the layout of their wheels but also by the height of their seats. The lower the seat, the greater their performance — the consequence of a lower centre of gravity and a reduction in frontal area which minimises aerodynamic drag. Machines with higher seats are slower around corners but they are easier to get in and out of, easier to use in traffic and often designed to carry more luggage.

The Tripod from LTE, uniquely, straddles performance and practicality with a medium height seat which behaves like a much lower machine because the rider's centre of gravity automatically moves with the steering.

The tripod leans like a bicycle, tilting into corners and this allows for greater speed and/or safety (depending on your priorities).

The Tripod is constructed from chromoly steel and aluminium and features rear wheel suspension for added comfort and control. LTE offer many options and purpose-made accessories, including a range of stock or custom colours and a choice of transmission types — from a nine speed derailleur to a Rohloff 14. And, for those who want it, they even make a non tilting version!

Anthrotech »

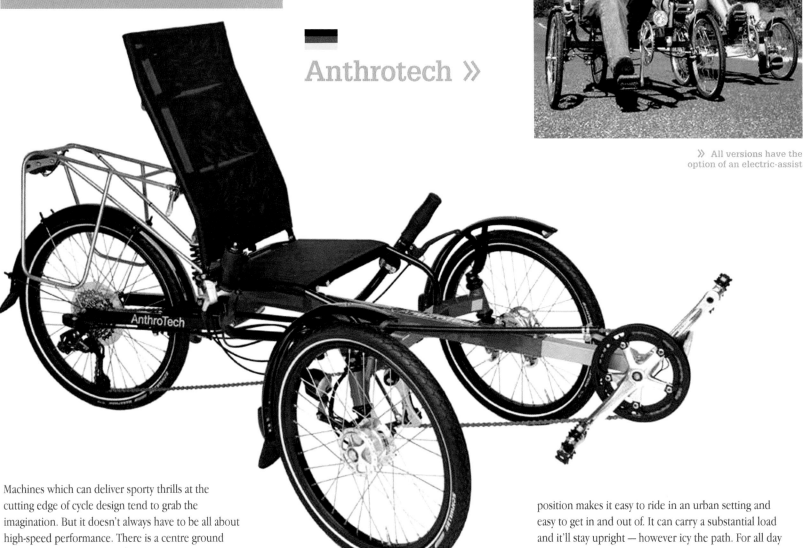

» All versions have the
option of an electric-assist

Machines which can deliver sporty thrills at the cutting edge of cycle design tend to grab the imagination. But it doesn't always have to be all about high-speed performance. There is a centre ground where you can find all of the benefits of a recumbent tricycle over a regular, upright, bicycle or tricycle — stability, surefootedness and comfort — but where you're not required to lie with your rear so near to the ground.

The Anthrotech won't be winning any races but that's not the point of it. A comfy seat with a commanding riding position makes it easy to ride in an urban setting and easy to get in and out of. It can carry a substantial load and it'll stay upright — however icy the path. For all day touring comfort or every day trips to the store there's little to beat it.

Machines such as this definitely deliver high performance. It just depends how we define the word.

Greenspeed Magnum »

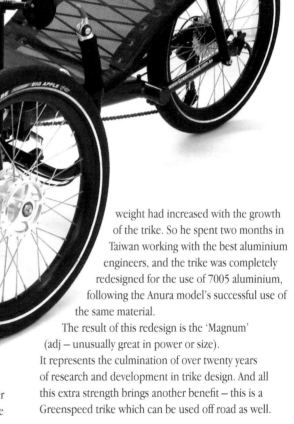

Ian Sim, CEO of Greenspeed Recumbents, was visiting a Greenspeed dealer in Jackson, Missouri when he witnessed a big guy struggling with one of his X5 trikes. It got him thinking about how the famous Greenspeed handling could be incorporated into a larger trike which would be also easier to get in and out of. It meant that he had to rethink many of his long-held notions of how a trike should look.

Many dealers had asked for 20" wheels, with a higher seat, to allow easy entry and exit, but Ian had resisted the idea, pointing out that it hurts the handing and road holding. So, how to fix it? Working on the Greenspeed principal, that three things are normally required for a proper fix, the front wheels were cambered to give extra stability without extra width, the cross member was 'veed' back to bring the seat closer to the standing rider's legs, and finally the seat was made adjustable for height as well as recline. It meant that if a rider lost weight through riding the trike, they would then be able to lower the seat, and gain the benefits of a lower centre of gravity. Cambering the front wheels, using a stronger rim section, and increasing the spoke count, enabled

the use of 20" (instead of the usual 16") wheels without compromising the strength.

The big surprise, once the first 'GT Plus' prototype was built in Australia, was that even with the seat height at 17 inches, the trike was far more stable than expected – and what's more it was faster than expected. However, Ian was not happy that the

weight had increased with the growth of the trike. So he spent two months in Taiwan working with the best aluminium engineers, and the trike was completely redesigned for the use of 7005 aluminium, following the Anura model's successful use of the same material.

The result of this redesign is the 'Magnum' (adj – unusually great in power or size). It represents the culmination of over twenty years of research and development in trike design. And all this extra strength brings another benefit – this is a Greenspeed trike which can be used off road as well.

Greenspeed
Anura »

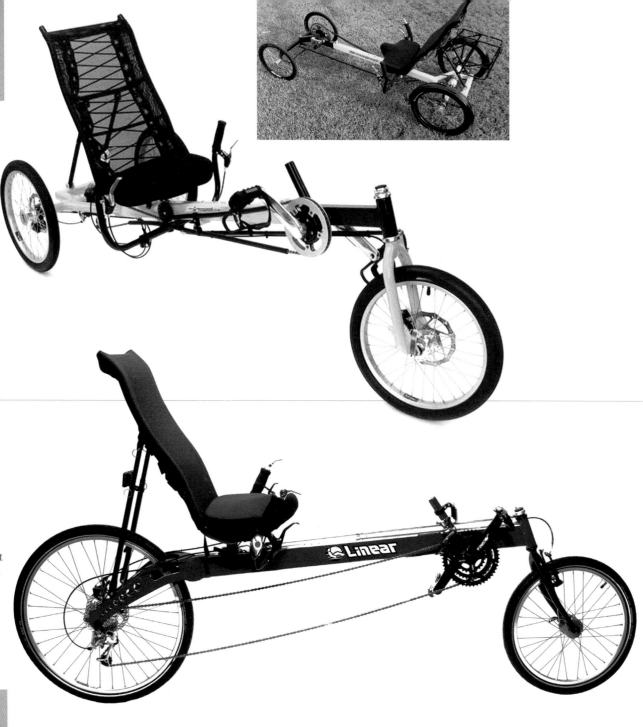

The Anura is a high quality, two wheel drive, user-friendly recreational tricycle for people who like to ride higher in traffic, and for senior or disabled riders who are unable to get up and down from low trikes. The delta format eliminates the cross member in front of the seat, making it easier to access, and having the wheel directly in front of the rider gives a greater sense of security in traffic. The Anura can be converted to a quadricycle with the substitution of the front sub-assembly, or a tandem with the tandem coupler.

Linear Limo »

A long wheel base bike is a slightly less manoeuvrable and a bit more stable than a short base bike. With less weight over the front wheel LWB bikes are easy to steer and they make great first recumbents. Linear recumbents have been around since the mid eighties. Originally manufactured in Iowa, they were light, comfortable and inexpensive and they sold like hot cakes. With a change of ownership, a move to a different state and some major technical improvements over the original, the new - New York state made - Linear is a big step up from the original, without losing any of the features which made it a success the first time around. Linear also make a short base bike called the Roadster.

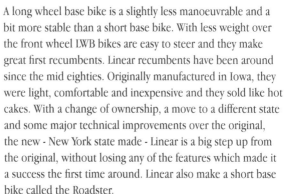

Szatuna Kft » ═
Carbon Recumbent

Increased comfort and reduced aerodynamic drag are the two primary selling points of recumbents, and it is for the buyer to decide which of these is the most important. But recumbents are not immune to the traditional wants of regular bikes: drive-train stiffness and low weight. Carbon-fibre composite construction can deliver some serious performance advantages for bicycles but the cost of investment in special tooling has been beyond the kind of small specialist manufacturers who produce recumbents. Until now. Enter Carbon Recumbents. With a background in carbon fibre composite construction for the automotive industry they were perfectly placed to bring this cutting edge construction technique to the cutting edge world of recumbent bicycles. The designer's aims were to minimise aerodynamic drag and optimise transmission efficiency in a comfortable, easy to ride bike. It's fast, and it's light. And it's very good looking.

Cruzbike Vendetta »

Front-wheel-drive fell out of fashion for a hundred years with the demise of the High Bicycle, but it makes a lot of sense for the recumbent riding position. Very few recumbent designers have been able to overcome the complications associated with steering and driving the same wheel.

The extra long chain runs of most recumbents add weight and can have a negative effect on drive-train performance unless managed by energy sapping rollers. With the goal of efficient, pain-free cycling Cruzbike's unique approach started with the back end of a regular road bike. The design delivers crisp shifts and good drive-train stiffness. This bike holds some serious speed and distance records. Cruzbike have definitely made it work.

The Mango » by Sinner Bikes

The Mango from Sinner has been around for a decade. It's based around a Quest recumbent tricycle and has seen many refinements. Though they differ in intent, velomobiles and competition focused Human Powered Vehicles share a lot of physics. The aerodynamic efficiency which allows humans to attain unfeasible speeds in competition is useful to a long range touring or commuting cyclist (who can also benefit from the excellent weather protection the fairing provides). Velomobile practicalities include greater ground clearance than outright speed machines, a smaller turning circle, easier access, storage and lights. But what they do share with their racing sisters, and where they really shine, is their speed advantage. They may not have the same outright velocity as land speed record machines but in a velomobile an ordinary rider can achieve average speeds of which a Tour de France peleton would be proud. They're not yet common enough to be cheap, and they are not as easy as a bicycle to live with, but a velomobile genuinely fills the gap between a bicycle and a private car. Without costing the earth. Sinner have a full range of unfaired recumbents too.

Sinner Comfort LWB Tricycle

Sinner Spirit SWB Recumbent Bicycle

The Outlaws

The world of HPV (Human Powered Vehicle) racing has developed in its own unpredictable ways, free from the design restrictions laid down by the regulators of mainstream cycle sport. There are no conventions, but instead a community of open-minded designers and riders competing for fun and a sense of achievement. The technology develops rapidly, fuelled by the sharing of experiences and knowledge, especially in aerodynamics. There are plenty of blind alleys, but also rapid advances. HPV racing is one of the few examples in the world of cutting edge technology arising from the enthusiasm and expertise of amateurs.

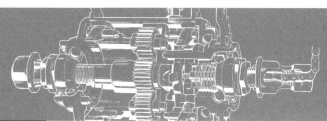

Transmissions in Focus »

Bicycle technology has always been about waiting for the fact to catch up with the fantasy – we want transmissions which are clean, lightweight, cheap, user-friendly, indestructible and which will last forever.

In the search for the ultimate drive-train many alternatives have been tried but chains are still pulling most power – even though they get filthy when lube gets contaminated by road dirt – or rusty when left unlubricated. Unless you enclose a chain in a chaincase oil bath it will eventually, inevitably, wear out. But the humble bicycle chain is famously and surprisingly efficient at transferring energy. It is also extremely well developed and almost universal – so anything which hopes to replace it had better outperform it on several levels.

Shaft drives are on the scene again. Though slightly less mechanically efficient than chains, they are clean and low-maintenance – but the bike's frame needs to be purpose-built around it.

Belt drives, too, require high levels of frame alignment accuracy, minimal frame flex – oh, and a gap in the frame through which the belt can be installed: there's no splitting belts like we do with chains. On the other hand belt drive gives significantly reduced rotating weight – clean, maintenance-free running and enhanced durability.

Posh Tranny »

NuVinci Continuously Variable Hub »

In the beginning was the crank arm attached to a wheel. Going faster was a matter of pedalling faster or building a bigger wheel, only limited by the length of the rider's legs. Stepping down from our penny farthings was a defining moment in our evolution. Rover's revolutionary 1885 'Safety' bicycle used different sized sprockets connected by a chain – allowing a high ratio without the dangerously high wheel.

We humans are less than wonderful engines – efficient but not very powerful, and we work only over a very narrow range of revolutions per minute. A single gear ratio is inexpensive and simple but it seriously compromises speed and hill-climbing ability unless the rider has enormous physical flexibility. Multiple gears allow us to pedal at a near-constant speed uphill or down dale. There aren't very many options when it comes to gears. You can use the chain running over multiple sprockets – with some kind of mechanism for de-railing the chain from one sprocket to the next. Or you can install a gear box somewhere, the most common location being within the rear hub itself. Neither system is new. And each type has settled down to a comfortable middle age. Broadly speaking more mechanically efficient derailleur systems are used for performance bikes whilst heavier internal gears are aimed at the utility end of the market.

Companies like Sturmey-Archer, Rohloff, SRAM and Shimano have raised the bar in recent years in the quality, efficiency and range of their hub gears – but the rise of the rear suspension bike and the associated desire to minimise un-sprung weight has turned technological attention towards frame-mounted gearboxes. As they move the weight from the centre of the wheel to the frame, gearboxes also address some of the other issues of derailleur gears – exposure to dirt and vulnerability to crash damage. It's not a new idea: manufacturers were producing bikes with frame-mounted gearboxes in the 1930s. Like shafts and belts they require a dedicated, purpose-built frame but the advantages are so clear that many companies are entering the field – Suntour, Pinion and G-Boxx among them. However, until mass-production kicks in they'll remain rare and expensive.

A resurgent Sturmey-Archer seems to produce another new and exciting niche gear hub every other week. Of particular interest are their S3X, a three-speed fixed-wheel hub, and their QS-RC5(W), a five-speed hub with built-in coaster brake, and automatic reverse! Pedal backwards from a standstill and back it goes. If you've ever pedalled a cargo tricycle you'll know why.

Two of the most interesting products of recent years are Schlumpf's neat retrofittable, heel-activated, bottom-bracket-mounted, two-speed gearbox – which doubles the number of gears of any non-derailleur bike. And NuVinci's wildly innovative CVP (continuously variable planetary).

Where Schlumpf has two widely-spaced gears the NuVinci has none. Instead of the steps of a conventional set of gears the NuVinci has a stepless ramp. It paves the way for a genuinely automatic pedelec transmission. It's arguably the most exciting technological innovation in bicycle transmissions since Rover's Safety bike. And, ironically, it's

Rohloff Speedhub 14 »

possibly the perfect gear system for the kind of utility cyclist who doesn't want to understand what's going on down there, but who just wants to get on and ride.

Current developments show ingenuity at its best, giving us more fascinating and useful options than ever before.

« Schlumpf Speed Drive ✚

An easy way of instantly doubling the number of gears on a one-speed or hub-gear-equipped bike. The unique Schlumpf two-speed system is shifted by pressing a button with the heel, eliminating shifters and cables. In the twenty years since Florian Schlumpf started production of his system the range has expanded to include three models, each with different spreads of gears, belt drive versions and even hubs for unicycles.

People, Bikes and Places »

The work of Sue Darlow, photographer of cycling and the life around it.

The great cycling photography captures – for a brief moment – a rich relationship between people, their bicycles and their place on the planet. One of the very best was Sue Darlow, whose thoughtful and varied work so enriched the cycling publishing world. Sue died of cancer in April 2011, at the age of 50. She was a good friend to many who are involved in Cyclorama.

Sue was half English and half Indian. Some of her finest non-cycling photography portayed the Parsi community she so loved. Her time in England was spent in Oxford, where she photographed a cycling culture which has changed little. She also spent part of her later life in Modena, Italy, where she chronicled the city's everyday cycling culture.

We publish here some of her images from our library: in memory of a remarkable person and her unique achievement.

» The school run in Bombay

» Sue Darlow and daugher Shehnaz at a Get Cycling Holiday

》 Clockwise from top left:
Picking up a trishaw from the city pound
Standing up for cycling in India
Morning sunshine, Oxford

Good and Bad »

Mick Allan looks at what makes a good bike good »

"There is hardly anything in the world that some man cannot make a little worse and sell a little cheaper, and the people who consider price only are this man's lawful prey."

John Ruskin

We like inexpensive bikes very much. Contrary to what some in the industry would have us believe you don't have to own a carbon fibre and titanium superbike to qualify as a 'cyclist'. A big part of cycling's appeal to new leisure riders and urban commuters is that it doesn't cost a fortune.

Inexpensive bikes are great. They deliver performance, durability and value for money to beat any other mode of transport for short journeys. But for anyone who intends to ride regularly, a cheap bike is never exactly that. Any money saved on the day of purchase will soon be cancelled out by repair bills and personal disruption as low quality components fail one by one.

But where is the line between 'inexpensive' and 'cheap'? I'm not sure I know, and if it's a tough call for a bike geek like me what hope does a newcomer have of sorting the good from the bad and the ugly?

Let's take a couple of familiar components as examples: bars and tyres. Our contact with the bike and the bike's contact with the road. There are thousands of different handlebars available, and between them, incremental differences in materials and processes. At the bottom of the pile are seam-welded painted or thinly plated steel bars. They are prone to rust, heavy and dull. At the other end: rare and exclusive sub-100gram carbon bars for lots of lolly. And somewhere between the sublime and ridiculous are the

workaday products. Decent, inexpensive, light-enough handlebars which simply do what they say on the box.

It's much the same story for every single component on a bike. Consumers pay more for better materials, more numerous and more complex manufacturing processes and for the research and development which delivers better performance, less weight and more durability.

Tyres too come in all shapes and sizes and at a range of price points. The ultimate bicycle tyre will have low rolling resistance, be impervious to punctures, grip like a demon, never wear out and cost only a few pennies. Unfortunately most of these performance parameters are mutually exclusive! Good grip is the enemy of durability. Puncture resistance compromises rolling resistance. Low cost cannot deliver low weight. Manufacturers juggle these parameters in the hope that their tyre or their handlebars are the ones with the ideal blend of features, performance and cost and the one you'll choose to fit to your bike.

The same applies to complete bikes. It's possible to compare two bikes from the same manufacturer, right next to each other in the range, and discover that they share no two components alike. Add $&50 to a retail price point

and sometimes everything changes: a slightly better bar, a slightly better saddle, one-step-up bearings with tighter seals, one more sprocket and so on. Perhaps even made in a different factory.

For the product manager who designed the supermarket bike, the cost of each component was the primary consideration, and very little good comes from building anything down to a price.

So where is this elusive line? The familiar mantra 'buy the best that you can afford' doesn't tell the whole story. Why spend a thousand if a bike costing a fraction of that will get the job done? Some commentators draw the line based on a artbitary price point: $&200/250 etc. But that's way too vague. It's certainly not enough simply to trust a brand whose name is familiar – what might have been considered among the best in the world a decade ago might be owned by a totally different parent company today. Making the effort to select the right type of bike for your needs will at least send you to the right sector of the market.

One way is to put the decision in the hands of the person selling the bike. Bike Geek at the Local Bike Shop is

unlikely to sell you a bad bike because he or she is probably a cyclist, and wants you to enjoy cycling, to continue doing it and keep going back to buy new tyres and lights and all the other essential doodads which keep the till ringing. A good salesperson will ask plenty of questions – to home in on what you need. Supermarket Check-out Person probably doesn't have an opinion either way.

Inexpensive, reliable, useful bicycles have the power to change our world. For less money than most people spend on car insurance they can have a bike which will give them years of trouble-free, low-cost transport, health, fitness and personal freedom.

Why should we care? Because cheap bikes are slow and uncomfortable. They are unreliable, prone to rust, their bearings wear out and their wheels become wobbly. They are difficult and frustrating to work on and to adjust. So cheap bikes spend much of their short brutal lives out of action, but worst of all, cheap bikes discourage people from cycling, because cheap bikes reinforce the false notion, at every turn of the pedals, that cycling is unpleasant. Bikes are one of those rare items were buying quality usually means buying happiness.

Love your Local Bike Shop »

Anyone who knows anything about buying a bicycle will tell you — the big question is not 'Which bike should I buy?' but 'Where should I buy it?'

Buying a first bike, or getting back into cycling after a time away, is a journey into unknown territory. To beginner cyclists, a bike shop — any bike shop - is a sea of wheels and strange looking accessories. With little or no experience, how are they to know the difference between a good bike and a bad bike? A good shop from a bad shop?

The sporting goods warehouse, the car accessories chain, the giant out-of-town toy store, the buy-now-pay-later mail-order catalogue and, these days, even supermarkets: they all sell 'bicycles'. The independent bike shop in town sells bicycles too, but their cheapest bike is twice as much as the bikes on the forecourt of the petrol station. It's entirely understandable that many people come to the conclusion that the local cycle shop caters only for cycling enthusiasts and the wealthy, not for ordinary people who just want to ride to work or pedal with the family at the weekend.

When you go to a proper bike shop you may be paying more at the till, but you will also receive more. You'll be advised by experts who are everyday cyclists themselves. They'll expose you to a greater selection of proper bikes and they'll give you real answers to your questions. They can also offer you maintenance advice, and are more likely to give you good after-sales service. At a proper bike store you will probably be able to test-ride, and buy a bike — the right bike, to last you decades. Above all, because a local shop cares whether you come back or not, you are less likely to be sold something inappropriate or which will give you long-term problems.

It is impossible to buy just a bicycle. You take home a machine which will, as you ride it and get to know it more, become a personal friend. The best friends will invariably come from bricks-and-mortar bike shops with real people behind them. People who sell cycles because they love cycling — people who will sell you the right bike because they want you to succeed not simply because they want to make a buck. Someone once said: "It's easy to make a small fortune — take a large fortune and open a bike shop with it." Margins are tight. No-one works in a bike shop for the money, not even the shop owner.

Clearly not every independent cycle shop deserves five stars and not every mega-store is bad. But each decision you make as to how and where you spend your money plays a part in the struggle of independent retailers of all kinds against the big multinationals. Life is not always easy for local bike shops but they are an important part of the local community and the local economy. We hope you'll support those which try a little harder.

From top »

Big and bold: Greggs Cycles in Bellevue, Seattle.

A bike shop in Rostock, then in the German Democratic Republic, photographed 1990 by Felix Ormerod

Mojo Bicycle Café in San Francisco

» A Tour de France celebration at Look Mum No Hands – a London bike shop and café. Photo: Robert Mason

» Get Cycling, a York bike shop which operates try-out roadshows and bike loan programmes. Here working with disabled customers.

» Workcycles in Amsterdam. Tom Resink Photography

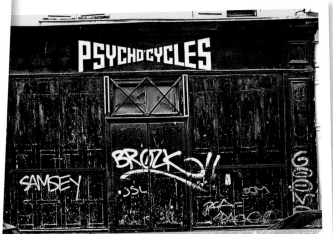

» Psychocycles – a defunct bike shop in Paris, with a certain ravaged timelessness. Photo by Jean Paul Margnac

Index »

These are the cycle-makers featured in this book. We show their country of origin, but almost all have distribution in many other countries. We also show their own website, as well the address at cyclorama.net where we have written extended profiles and described their other bikes.

Ryan Heyne: 6.
www.streetscenespdx.com

Get Cycling photolibrary: 16 to 19, 74, 101 lower, 104, 118, 119, 122 lower right, 131 lower left, 15. www.getcycling.org.uk.

Sue Darlow: 20, 44 left, 55, 65 lower right, 75 top, all of 152 and 153.

David Eccles: 40, 41.

C-Reel (Heritage image, b/w) 27 www.C-reel.com

Ade Adjou and Paul Boussarie (Heritage image) 28 left.

Merida Bicycles: 28, 29, 30, 43 far right, 110, 121

Jason Patient: 31, 42 top left, 42 right, 43 lower right. All 45, all 62 all 63, 64, 65 left, 100 right, 122 lower left, 123 upper, 128 upper left. 131 Top left and bottom right. 140. 160: 3rd, 4th, 5th 6th and 9th pictures. 161. www.cycling-images.co.uk.

British Cycling: 34, 116 top.

Robin Thom: 38, all of 87 and 87, 159. www.robinthom.photoshelter.com

Stephen McKay: 39

Peter Gostelow: 43 middle. www.petergostelow.com

Kimura, Hungary: 43, centre.

Rahsaan Bahati. 42 upper centre. www.bahatifoundation.org

Jim McGurn: 44 middle, 65 centre, 85 left, 89 bottom, 96 top, 97, 105 left, 149 bottom left and bottom right, 157 top. 160 top right, lower centre and bonfire.

Brompton Bicycle: 57

Marc van Woudenberg: 73. www.amsterdamize.com

Velovision: 75 lower right. www.velovision.com

Jonathan Maus: 80, 100 left. 162. www.bikeportland.org

Mark Panama: 81 left

Brien Henderson: 81 right

Team Rwanda: 82, 83

Henry Cutler Workcycles: 84 top right & bottom left. www.workcycles.com

Thomas Resink Photography: 8 to 9, 67, 131, 157 bottom left. www.tomresink.com

Spezialradmesse Germersheim: 85 top

Fahrradhof Berlin: 85 right

Cycle Embassy Copenhagen: 88 and 89 top

Yakkay Helmets: 89 centre

Tim Hall: 90 top

British Cycling: 90 centre

Dean Askin: 91 centre

Sam Witteringham: 91 right, top and bottom

Brent Curry: 91 bottom left.

Stephen Crawford: 92

Ben Torode: 93 right. www.flickr.com/photos/bentorode

Kinya Hanada: 94 left

Cycleangelo, Yamaguchi US team bike: 95 top. www.cycleangelo.cc

Mary Ann Hooper: 95

Dominic J. R. Hammond: 98 lower

Dom Mason: 113 main image

Szymon Nieborak: 113 inset image

Adrien Hamm: 106

Cooper Brownlee: 108 and 109 lower

Spencer Moret (Pure): 108 top right

Sarah Feord: 117

Simon Keitch: 120, 122 upper. www.simonkeitch.com

Alan Towse: 129

Maderna: 134

Bernds: 135

Flyer/Movelo: 136, 137

Rose Hulman: 149 top. www.rose-hulman.edu/hpv

Recumbents.com: 149

British Human Power Club: 149 www.bhpc.org.uk

Gregg's Cycles: 156 top

Felix Ormerod: 156 centre

Mojo Bicycle Café 156 bottom: www.mojobicyclecafe.com

Robert Mason: 157 top left. www.robertwmason.co.uk

Jean Paul Margnac: 157 bottom right

David Bocking: 158

Cyclorama Week

Cyclorama Week is an annual, international, residential spokefest for anyone who love bikes and riding them: cycle designers, makers, philosophers, historians, retailers, and anyone who want to join in the buzz. People from all walks of life, of all ages, and with very varied tastes in bikes. Guided bike rides, try-out sessions, activities for children, demos, talks, films: if you like Cyclorama you'll enjoy Cyclorama Week. These Weeks began over 15 years ago, and are run by Company of Cyclists, publishers of Cyclorama. They have taken place in the UK, France, Germany and the Netherlands, under various names. For details visit

www.cyclorama.net/cycloramaweek

CYCLORAMA

Publisher Information »

Published by Company of Cyclists Ltd.
Edited, written and produced by Jim McGurn and Mick Allan.
Systems and Administration: Miark
Case study and picture research: Dominic J R Hammond Esquire
Website programming: Semlyen IT (www.semlyen.net)
Logistical support and bike handling: Get Cycling CiC (www.getcycling.org.uk)
Original design is by Biskit (www.biskit.co.uk)
Production design is by Bob Main of Frozen Marrow (www.frozenmarrow.com)
Our thanks to George Goodwin, Camilla (Kimberly) Wimberley, Sally McGurn, Rob Ainsley

How Cyclorama works
Cyclorama is owned and financed by 190 cyclist-supporter shareholders from around the world.
Our aim is to reflect and promote the richness of international cycle culture. The book is only part
of the story. We have put a hundred times as much material on www.cyclorama.net, where you
can also find out more about the cycle-makers featured in the case studies, and discover more of
their products. To help finance the book and website we have asked the cycle-makers in the case
studies to make a small financial contribution. This has help cover some of our early costs. They
are there by invitation: we have been very selective, in terms of how special and interesting we
find the cycle and its maker.

Our Thanks
We have been overwhelmed by the support we have received for this project: from cyclists,
cycling organisations and participants worldwide. It has reminded us that if you're among
cyclists you're among friends. We are particularly grateful for the indispensible role played by
our many patient cyclist-shareholders. Their long-term finance gave us the time to make our
mistakes then, hopefully get things right.

Cyclorama Shop:
Copies of this book, Jim McGurn's history book; *On Your Bicycle,* and other high
quality Cyclorama merchandise is available to order via the Cyclorama on-line shop:
www.cyclorama.net/shop

Cyclorama Worldwide:
Cyclorama is written and designed for a worldwide readership. We are appointing
Cyclorama distributors in many countries, and will be producing several editions of this
book, some in other languages. If you are interested in becoming an agent, dealer, distributor
or co-publisher please contact us. All up-to-date information on international availability,
distribution and foreign language rights can be found at www.cyclorama.net/worldsales.

The Next Cyclorama
We will publish the second international edition (Cyclorama 2) in due course. If you want us
to alert you when published, email admin@cyclorama.net, and we'll let you know.

Environmental
This book was printed by Cambrian Printers Ltd, Aberystwyth, Wales, using vegetable-based
inks, on alcohol-free presses, and using chemical-free plates. The paper is entirely from sources
accredited by the Forestry Stewardship Council.

Contact:
Company of Cyclists, 3 Acaster Estate, Acaster Malbis, York YO23 2TX UK
Email: admin@cyclorama.net Tel: 00 (44)1904 706700

Cyclorama is distributed in the UK by Gazelle Books.

www.cyclorama.net

The Cyclorama website is a huge and growing international
resource. If you like the book you'll more than like the website.
One function of the website is to tell you lots more about the cycle
makers appearing in the book, and their products.

A bicycle can mean anything to anybody. It allows us to slip in and out of other people's expectations, conventions and transportation systems. We can go off riding almost anytime, anywhere, and on anything from a scrapheap challenge to a titanium miracle machine.

Our bicycles give us free will. We can escape and engage as we wish, harming no-one. Ours is the freedom of the minimal — because less is more.

When you have finished reading this book, please place it in the hands of someone who doesn't ride a bike.